THE HEART OF THE GOSPEL

By the same author

CHRIST AND BAHÁ'U'LLÁH

THE GLAD TIDINGS OF BAHÁ'U'LLÁH

THE MISSION OF BAHÁ'U'LLÁH

THE PROMISE OF ALL AGES

THE HEART OF THE GOSPEL

or

The Bible and the Bahá'í Faith

By

GEORGE TOWNSHEND, M.A. (Oxon.)

Sometime Canon of St. Patrick's Cathedral, Dublin

Archdeacon of Clonfert

GEORGE RONALD

OXFORD

GEORGE RONALD, Publisher
46 High Street, Kidlington, Oxford, United Kingdom
OX5 2DN

First published by Lindsay Drummond Ltd., 1939
Second Edition, revised and enlarged,
published by George Ronald 1951
Reprinted 1955
Talisman Edition 1960
Hardcover Edition 1972
This Edition 1995

ISBN 0-8598-020-9

Printed in Great Britain by
the Alden Press, Oxford

CONTENTS

PUBLISHER'S NOTE

Mr. Townshend used three versions of the Bible: the King James, the Revised, and the Moffatt translation. It has seemed fitting to retain his quotations in forms familiar to him.

In these days when the truths of Christianity are diluted and compromised to fit the notions of an age admittedly unbelieving, this classic work on the Bible and the Bahá'í Faith speaks compellingly to those who cannot forget the deepest truths in which they were reared, and likewise to those who, deprived of religion in childhood and youth by elders who had forsaken it, yet sense their loss, their ignorance of purpose, the hollowness of days spent only for material benefit.

George Townshend possessed a supreme trust in God, the Creator and Sustainer of all life. His book mirrors his profound contemplation of this central Mystery, his poet's joy in all Its manifestations, a believer's confidence which nothing was able to deflect. He wrote to awaken us to these realities.

INTRODUCTION

This essay endeavours to follow the guidance of Bahá'u'lláh back to Christ and to let the light of the Gospel shine in its ancient purity upon the darkness of our time. It is conceived and written in the firm belief that any Christian who reaches the heart of the Gospel and understands the true exaltation of Christ will soon discover the way that lies open, through Bahá'u'lláh, to the reunion of the Christian Churches, the re-Christianising of the West, and the regeneration of the human race.

The Bible bears witness that history in its essence is a spiritual thing and cannot be rightly understood except from a spiritual point of view. Realistic as the sacred narrative is, exposing freely all the weakness and wickedness of mankind, it maintains always the spiritual attitude. It never modifies its opening words: '*In the beginning, God*'. It shows that the forces which impel history and the laws that govern it, its origin and its ultimate issue, all belong to the spiritual realm. It reveals in human events the presence of a universal continuity which flows on for ever, as a mysterious divine Will works out its gradual purpose upon the surface of the planet.

The true beginnings of the Gospel are not to be found within the limits of the New Testament. They reach back through the length of the Bible to the Pentateuch, to the time of Moses and of Abraham and beyond. They are involved in the design of Creation itself. And its end is revealed only in those prophecies and promises which fill the closing chapters of the Scripture and which through all the vicissitudes of these intervening centuries have warmed the hearts of Christians with expectancy and hope.

If we are to follow the example of the Bible in dealing with the problems of our time, we will regard first their spiritual aspect and will search out the spiritual issues that are at stake, since upon these the material issues depend. We shall be prepared to trace the causes of to-day's events far back through modern and mediæval times to spiritual energies released by our eternal Father in distant centuries.

In His teaching, and particularly in His *Book of Certitude*,* Bahá'u'lláh makes it clear that the Bible was given to mankind for the same purpose as that for which the Gospel was preached: to prepare humanity that they might recognise, appreciate, and use with wisdom the supreme crisis which He foresaw, and in which we find ourselves involved to-day, when, standing at the apex of the corporate history of mankind, we are in a position of unprecedented danger and also of unprecedented opportunity. Bahá'u'lláh explained that the perplexity of our world-leaders, their inability to master the problems of the era or tell whence these problems came or why they came or whither they lead or what they mean, is ultimately due to a moral and spiritual cause. It springs from a misunderstanding of the Gospel, and a misinterpretation of the symbolism and the abstruse terms in which many of

* *Kitáb-i-Íqán.* (Trans. by Shoghi Effendi. London: Bahá'í Publishing Trust. 2nd ed. 1961.)

its prophecies, promises, warnings and pronouncements are veiled. This figurative language of Scripture is a touchstone by which God distinguishes and rewards the true-hearted and the sincere. It yields up its real significance not to human learning, as is commonly supposed, but to an open and unprejudiced mind, to a pure and devout spirit which seeks the truth for love of God.

> . . . Man *He writes* can never hope to attain unto the knowledge of the All-Glorious, can never quaff from the stream of divine knowledge and wisdom, can never enter the abode of immortality, nor partake of the cup of divine nearness and favour, unless and until he ceases to regard the words and deeds of mortal men as a standard for the true understanding and recognition of God and His Prophets. (p. 3)

'Abdu'l-Bahá, expounding this truth, spoke often in the West of the profound importance, and the difficulty, of reaching a true interpretation of Scripture and urged His hearers to learn from the errors of the past. He expressed Himself, for instance, in the following words to a Bible-class in New York City:

> I have been informed that the purpose of your class meeting is to study the significances and mysteries of the holy scriptures and understand the meaning of the divine testaments. It is a cause of great happiness to me that you are turning unto the kingdom of God, that you desire to approach the presence of God and to become informed of the realities and precepts of God.

It is my hope that you may put forth your most earnest endeavour to accomplish this end; that you may investigate and study the holy scriptures word by word so that you may attain knowledge of the mysteries hidden therein. Be not satisfied with words but seek to understand the spiritual meaning hidden in the heart of the words. The Jews read the Old Testament night and day, memorising its words and texts, yet without comprehending a single meaning or inner significance; for had they understood the real meaning of the Old Testament they would have become believers in His Holiness Christ, inasmuch as the Old Testament was revealed to prepare His coming. As the Jewish doctors and rabbis did not believe in His Holiness it is evident that they were ignorant of the real significance of the Old Testament. It is difficult to comprehend even the words of a philosopher; how much more difficult it is to understand the words of God.*

How far the Christian Churches have wandered from a true understanding of the Gospel may be judged from the argument of this book. We are living in the Day of God which Christ announced and for which He prepared men's souls; and yet not one among the illustrious learned leaders of the Churches has proved capable of recognising it or has troubled to examine the claims of Bahá'u'lláh when these were drawn to his attention.

How disastrous may be the results of trusting to human learning rather than to a spiritual mind and a pure heart

* *The Promulgation of Universal Peace.* Vol. II, pp. 454–5. (Chicago: Baha'i Publishing Committee, 1925.)

for a true interpretation of Scripture may be seen from the fate of Jewry after its rejection of Jesus Christ, or from the humiliations of the Christian Church when it turned away from its Lord on His return.

CHAPTER I

THE BIBLE AS UNIVERSAL HISTORY

The Bible is a study in world-history. It is man's first effort to write a complete history of the human race from its beginning to its climax in the unification of all peoples and the establishment of a universal religion.

Though it was written so long ago, compiled under unfavourable conditions, though as a history it is neither exhaustive nor comprehensive, nor orderly in form nor scholarly in tone and manner; yet in spite of its handicaps it presents to the soul of man the most sublime and magnificent conception of the whole human race as being in reality one family whose history, however complex, is a continuous movement towards a single and all-sufficient consummation. Perhaps nothing will fully satisfy the heart and mind of thoughtful men save this vision of the oneness of the life of the race, and of an Eternal Will guiding all things towards an event in which an ever-advancing civilisation finds at last completeness and fulfilment.

Here in this ancient book, come down to us from primitive times and offered through the Authorised Version in befitting language of matchless power and beauty, this conception is set forth with a clearness and a force which has not weakened through the ages and with a fullness of meaning which no epoch has been so well able to appreciate as ours.

The early chapters of Genesis are universal in their

outlook. They take a general survey of the whole earth and of all its inhabitants. They tell of Adam and Eve, the progenitors of the whole human race, and of the three sons of Noah, Shem, Ham and Japheth ('of them was the whole earth overspread'). They describe how 'the whole earth was of one language, and of one speech' until God confounded men's language and 'did scatter them abroad upon the face of the whole earth'. In the twelfth chapter the field of the narrative narrows, the action no longer embraces the whole human race, but centres henceforth round the fortunes of one people only, 'the chosen people' as they called themselves, the Hebrews, the descendants of Abraham. For a period of some two thousand years the history of mankind is seen through Jewish eyes and written from the Jewish point of view. The sacred narrative tells of the vicissitudes, the glories, the tragedies of the Hebrews. It traces their growth from a single family to a great and opulent nation and follows them through their subsequent decline and humiliation. But it does not give them this extraordinary prominence for their own sake, because of any native superiority of theirs to the rest of mankind. The Bible is not a nationalistic work. No one reading it could imagine the Hebrews enjoyed their distinction because they were really greater or dearer to God than any other people. Their failings are not extenuated; their conduct is not idealised nor eulogised. Their iniquities are frankly displayed. Their unworthiness of their blessings is mercilessly exposed. They call forth from the prophets the most scathing and tremendous denunciations. They occupy in the Bible a central place because they are, for a time, in an especial sense the trustees of God's universal purpose. The main subject of the Bible does not change in the twelfth chapter of Genesis, nor is the great theme ever forgotten. The thread of universal history runs through Jewish history. The tides of world-progress lap for a time round the shores of Palestine. At the very beginning of the Jewish race, in the wording of the call of Abraham, this universal outlook and purpose is proclaimed, 'I will make of thee a great nation . . . and in thee shall all families of the earth be blessed'. If through the exclusiveness of the Jew the oneness of the human race and of its progress is in any passage of the Bible obscured, it is never forgotten by Him who is the inspirer and true author of the Word of God.

Had the Jews accepted Christ, they might still have retained a central place of responsibility in the history of mankind. The universal theme might still have been carried forward in the New Testament through Jewish history as it was in the Old Testament. But the Jews failed. They knew not the time of their visitation. The children of the Kingdom were cast out and others inherited their privileges. After the Crucifixion the Jews no longer march in the van of universal history. They fall aside from the main current of human progress. The cause of religion is advanced and the purpose of God goes forward—but not through the agency of the Jews. The high trusteeship they had held so long is forfeited and passes from them to the Gentiles. In the latter part of the New Testament the action spreads rapidly outward from Palestine to Ephesus and Macedonia and Athens, to Corinth and to Rome, till finally in the closing chapters of the Bible it embraces in prophetic survey the entire earth and all the peoples that inhabit it.

> And I saw a new heaven and a new earth . . . and I . . . saw the holy city, new Jerusalem, coming down from God out of heaven . . . And the nations of them which are saved shall walk in the light of it: and the kings of the earth do bring their glory and honour into it . . . In the midst of the street of it . . . *was there* the tree of life . . . and the leaves of the tree were for the healing of the nations. (Rev. xxi and xxii.)

Christ emphasised the universality and the unifying purposes of His Message. He bade His disciples 'go teach all nations'. He predicted that a certain deed of kindness done to Him would be remembered wherever the Gospel was preached in the wide world, and He announced that the close of His Age would not come till His Teaching had been carried to the ends of the earth. He said, moreover, that His Gospel was to soften and remove those estrangements among men caused by differences of race, nation, tradition or culture; it was to harmonise men's hearts and induce a sense of fellowship; and some day the whole of humanity would be gathered into one and become as a single flock of sheep under a single shepherd.

The Bible sketches world-history; but the spirit in which this theme is conceived and the point of view from which it is written are not those taken by the modern historian. The Bible regards the history of the human race as being from beginning to end in reality one and single. However rich in incident may be the onward movement of mankind, however complex it may be in action, however manifold in interest: though men may have lost their bearings altogether, though they may have forgotten their original unity and may have no conception of the ultimate goal towards which they are being carried, nevertheless the course of their progress flows all in one direction and is guided by a principle of unity which persists through all divisive influences and sooner or later will make its dominant power manifest.

The first picture presented in the Bible is that of human unity in its simplest form: that of a single family. The last picture is that of a unity manifold and universal in which all kindreds and tongues and peoples and nations are gathered into one and unified in the enjoyment of a common worship, a common happiness, a common glory.

The great problem which, according to the Bible, confronts the human race in its progress is that of advancing from the barest, baldest unity through a long experience of multiplying diversities till ultimately a balance between the two principles is struck, poise is gained and the two forces of variety and unity are blended in a multiple, highly developed world fellowship, the perfection of whose union was hardly suggested in the primitive simplicity of early man.

CHAPTER II

HISTORY AS SPIRITUAL EVOLUTION

The history of the whole human race, of all its tribes and nations and languages, from the beginning to the end, is—declares the Bible—one story.

But it is not one simply because the earth is one home, or simply because there is one root human race, or because the incidents of all history tend to a common consummation: nor for any reasons such as these alone. World-history is a single story for yet another and a far deeper kind of reason. World history has a single theme, and it is controlled throughout by a single divine thought. All things that occur—whatever be their date and whereever be the scene—are in some way related to that theme; and on the nature of their relation depends their value or their lack of value, their being constructive or destructive, progressive or retrogressive.

World-history at its core and in its essence is the story of the spiritual evolution of mankind. From this all other activities of man proceed and round it all other activities revolve. The Bible makes the tracing of this evolution its own special subject and writes world-history from this and from no other point of view. It sketches the spiritual development of the human race from its earliest infancy to the time of its maturity and represents this movement as being the main and central current of advancing civilisation and of all human progress. The life of humanity may be regarded in other aspects; world-history may be written from other points of view. The Bible itself is in a measure a general history, deals with many social and institutional changes, records the economic and political growth of the Hebrews, and is a storehouse of information on ancient customs and modes of life. But it treats these matters as incidental, as forming the environment or being the expression of the major theme of spiritual expansion and advance, and it asserts that this treatment answers to the real truth of things and preserves the just proportions of the world as God made it. Man's spiritual evolution is the true business and meaning of his existence; on their connection with this all other matters depend for the reality of their value. Any picture of human life which does not preserve this perspective but represents something else (such as wealth or conquest or reputation or pleasure or comfort or culture) as having in itself an independent importance is based on a misunderstanding and bears witness to untruth.

The Bible contains no word for evolution; yet evolution is its subject from beginning to end. The theme of evolution supplies the plot of the story, giving to it direction and purpose. It not only imparts to the long narrative continuity, massiveness and a sublime simplicity, but also reveals the intellectual coherence and order which are present in the unfolding of the grand redemptive design of God.

All men everywhere fall within the scope of this vast evolutionary movement: no one is left outside at any time anywhere. All men are alike and of like worth in that they are sprung from one root-race, are of one spiritual origin, and are held inescapably within this world-wide spiritual process. All the events of history, however multifarious, are when taken together items in a plot of universal spiritual development which, however complex in appearance, is in its inmost essence and its purpose utterly simple.

Devotees of literalism may proclaim the defects they have found in the Bible, and warn us that it has for us to-day no value as history or as philosophy or even perhaps—throughout great lengths of it—as religion. Yet the spiritual mind will in humility seek instruction from those inspired seers of old, will wonder at their strong faith, at the glory of their vision, at the depth and height of that understanding of the ways and the wisdom of God which by sheer spiritual power they attained. If we can divine their secret, if we can interpret our modern knowledge in terms of the Bible, what hidden wisdom may not be revealed to us, what victory and dominion may not be within our reach!

To read the Bible as a single work, using one part to supplement or to illumine the meaning of another, is to perceive that it sets forth creation as a continuous process of evolution which works up through the material realm to the spiritual and which moves forward without break or cessation or any stated end.

All that is hereafter to appear is in the beginning present to the thought of the Eternal Creator, and in that sense creation is carried through immediately to its completion by the fiat of the word of God. But all that is, and is to come, is not made manifest in this actual realm at once. At first, it is hidden. 'Hidden that it may be revealed', as the Lord Christ said. It is involved in the first act of creation; for with God there is no incompleteness: it is mysteriously folded away, as a tree with its branches, leaves and fruit is folded within the seed from which it is to spring.

At the foundation of the world all that the future contains already exists before God on the timeless plane of eternity. His full purpose in every detail is at the beginning defined, through however many degrees of slow development God may will it to unfold its length on this lower level of time wherein man dwells.

Evolution is—in the Bible—a mode of creation chosen by God, and it is not shown as ever reaching a final end. It was in movement through all the period when the Bible was being written and when the narrative of the Bible was being enacted: it is in movement now. The grand dénouement of the Bible, the Descent of the City of Peace, does not bring it to a close; but opens a new and more glorious chapter of civilisation before mankind. By slow degrees God moulds simple matter into complex forms, and by slow degrees he grants to man the privilege of self-knowledge and the power which flows from it.

The spiritual evolution of man is the main topic and interest of the Bible. But the narrative does not open with this topic, nor yet with man himself. It tells of the antecedents of man, and of the preparation that was made for him before he appeared upon the earth in person. It tells of the material world and of the lower kingdoms, animal, vegetable, mineral, of the sun and the moon and the stars, of Original Chaos and Old Night out of which Kosmos was formed. It tells how the natural world was brought into being step by step, stage after stage, by successive commands of the Creator and through a regular and ordered process.

Age after age through unnumbered millenniums the

Creative Will working in the immensities of space brought at last into being this earth, and with an unwearied, unhurrying patience wrought matter into form after form, each form more complex, more expressive than the last, till at length there was evolved the form of man.

To man, God gave dominion over the earth and all that it contained, 'over the fish of the sea and over the fowl of the air and over every living thing that moveth upon the earth'. He was to subdue the earth and to establish his conquest over nature.

For man was the last and consummate work of creation. He was the foreseen goal and end for which the heavens and the earth had been made and to which the whole process of evolution had led up. So perfect was his form, the last and finest flower of evolution, that God could breathe into it as into no lower form a breath of His own being. He could make it a tabernacle of the Holy Spirit. In it might dwell one like unto God Himself, endowed with the fullness of the divine perfections.

> And God said, Let us make man in our image, after our likeness: and let them have dominion over the fish of the sea, and over the fowl of the air, and over the cattle, and over all the earth, and over every creeping thing that creepeth upon the earth. So God created man in his *own* image, in the image of God created he him; male and female created he them. . . . And the Lord God formed man *of* the dust of the ground, and breathed into his nostrils the breath of life; and man became a living soul. (Gen. i and ii.)

God therefore needed to go no further in His work of moulding simple matter into structures. He did not need to make any spiritual mirror to reflect more perfectly the image of His beauty. Evolution had achieved its purpose, and God laid by His task.

But in the same moment He assumed another task. He rested from one labour to enter on another yet more exalted and wonderful. For if in the birth of man upon the earth material evolution ends, in that same birth spiritual evolution begins.

At this point the Bible takes up its main subject. All that had been accomplished by the Creator before was preliminary; and the Scripture summarised it in two pages—but twelve hundred pages are not enough to tell of the work which God began when He rested from the creation of the material world.

Henceforth God deals with man and with none other. The waters and the grass and the trees and the fowl and the whales and the cattle no longer play the most prominent part in the narrative. They sink for ever into the background. They become the environment of man and no more. God does not now give commands to the firmament nor to the waters, nor bestow His blessings on the fishes and the fowls, bidding them be fruitful and multiply. His command and His blessings henceforth are for mankind. But man is not regarded as akin to the lower animals. He is immeasurably superior to them. He is altogether apart and distinct from them and that which makes him thus distinct is the subject of scriptural history.

Man is a spirit. It is spirit which distinguishes him from an animal and constitutes his manhood. He is in touch with spiritual forces. He inhabits a spiritual realm. Any evolution or destiny that awaits him is in its nature spiritual. Connected on his animal side with that material world through which he has come into being, he is in Scripture not less closely connected with the spiritual world wherein God dwells. When the name of man is first mentioned in the Bible this twofold nature is affirmed, and it is assumed throughout the rest of Scripture. Often it is expressly stated, as in Eccles. xii. 7, 'Then,' says the Preacher, speaking of man's death, 'shall the dust return to the earth as it was: and the spirit shall return unto God Who gave it.' 'The spirit is willing,' said Christ, 'but the flesh is weak.'

Creation in every phase is in Scripture an act of the spirit of God—'the spirit of God moved upon the face of the waters.' (Gen. i. 2.) 'Thou sendest forth thy spirit, they are created . . .' (Ps. civ. 30.) 'Then saith the Lord God . . . he that spread forth the earth, and that which cometh out of it; he that giveth breath unto the people upon it, and spirit to them that walk therein.' (Isa. xlii. 5.)

But man, because of his unique spiritual status, has a special kind of dependence upon that spiritual power. In times of stress and crisis or for any supreme achievement, whether the need be spiritual or merely physical, a human being who is a true servant of God will receive special aid from on high. The Spirit of the Lord will help the faithful in battle.

It was not in his own strength that David slew Goliath, nor that Gideon delivered the Israelites from the Midianites—'the spirit of the Lord came upon Gideon . . .' (Judges vi. 34.) It is the spirit of the Lord which inspires the prophet: 'the Lord God, and his spirit, hath sent me,' says Isaiah (Isa. xlviii. 16); and Ezekiel likewise says, 'The hand of the Lord was upon me, and carried me out in the spirit of the Lord . . .' (Ezek. xxxvii. 1); St. Paul (I Cor. ii.

10 ff.) states that it is through spiritual communion with the Spirit of God that the believer is enabled to discern and understand spiritual things which cannot be understood by the natural man.

But this is not to say that primitive man in his original condition is in a spiritual sense a complete and finished product. Though he is made in the image of his Maker, though he is inspired by the Spirit of God and is pronounced by God to be very good: he is with not less definiteness and emphasis shown as being in fact very bad. 'Ye then being evil,' said Christ of mankind, assuming human wickedness as a thing for granted.

Scripture throughout bears witness to the manifold infirmities and imperfections of men. Adam and Eve both sinned. Their eldest son murdered his brother. Of the days of Noah it is written that 'God saw that the wickedness of *man* was great in the earth, and *that* every imagination of the thoughts of his heart *was* only evil continually. And it repented the Lord that he had made man on the earth, and it grieved him at his heart.' (Gen. vi. 5–6.)

Though the Bible never modifies its original statement that man is made in the image of God, yet almost every book contains the record of sin and utters laments over its prevalence.

Over against everything that is fair and true and noble stands that which is base and false and cruel. The conflict between good and evil rages incessantly; the issue seems always uncertain. Again and again the hosts of darkness triumph. The fierceness of the struggle does not lessen with the passage of centuries. To the end, sin does not relax its grip on men's hearts. Secular literature can hardly contain a more terrible indictment of the depravity of human nature than that written by St. Paul in the first chapter of his Epistle to the Romans.

Men may be made in the image of God, yet (as the Bible presents it) the history of the tribes and peoples and nations of the world, of the Hebrews and the Gentiles, reflects at no time the order and harmony and the happiness of a divine world. It is a tale of turmoil and vicissitude, of struggle and trouble, of sorrow and loneliness and penitence, of bitter shame, and hopes lost and hearts broken.

Men dream of heaven and peace, they long for a better order of things than that which they have made. Prophetic promises of a great felicity, of a sure deliverance from the fears of life, and from its discords and its wrongs and its despairs, buoy up the fainting hearts of the generations and grow with the passing centuries more full and clear. But no nation ever walks with a whole heart in the ways of God or in the sunshine of His presence; by the multitudes happiness is only seen if at all in faint and far-off glimpses; the joys of heaven and the sweetness of divine love are the privilege of a few rare, outstanding souls. After two thousand years of specially vouchsafed training the children of Abraham commit the most heinous of all the crimes recorded in the Bible and bring down upon their heads the most awful of all punishments. At the close of the whole narrative, the everlasting promise of a new heaven and a new earth, of the subjugation of evil and the world-wide reign of truth and justice, remains still a distant prospect, deferred beyond the end of the Christian Era and only to be fulfilled when the power of the Father reinforces that of Christ returned in glory.

But the spiritual eye perceives that in spite of appearances, Evil throughout the Bible history never can meet Good on its own ground. Evil stands on a lower level; it lacks the reach and the substantiality of the power of the Good. For all its display of force and for all the suffering it causes, it is not in reality positive. It is in the nature of a shadow which, however deep its darkness, is only a shadow, dependent for its existence on the absence of light. The darkness cannot go forth and challenge the day. The glory of heaven is never stained by the glooms of hell; God's dominion is never challenged. The final defeat of Evil, which from very early days is promised to man, is assured from the foundation of the world by the very constitution of things. A happy ending to the history of man is from the beginning assured by the might of the One Sovereign Will who brought all things into existence.

The postponement of the triumph of virtue and of the Descent of the New Jerusalem is not due to any lack of power on God's part, nor to any arbitrary fiat. The seeming delay is a necessary part of the creational process. Evil does not intrude itself upon the divine scheme from some outside source; it falls within the divine scheme. From the first, it is foreseen and aforedoomed. It represents an original lack, a shortcoming, which man has to rise out of and to outgrow. The long postponement of humanity's happiness is, for all the sorrow it entails, recognised by the spiritual mind to be a bounty of the All Merciful flowing from His love and His care for His creatures.

Man's upward movement out of spiritual incompleteness has its parallel and antetype in the story of the gradual creation of the world in the six days. Until material evolution reached its climax in the birth of man, imperfection reigned everywhere over land and sea. Fishes existed and ferns, and reptiles and birds, and the like; but there was as yet no form capable of registering the higher spiritual impulses; the purpose for which creation had been undertaken was unattained and undiscernible; and it was not until long ages after the body of man appeared, that the meaning of the process at last became evident and material evolution achieved a perfect result.

The period of world history covered by the Bible corresponds to the five and a half days in the creation-story before the appearance of man. As there was then everywhere on the planet material imperfection and incompleteness, and nothing else; so likewise has there been spiritual imperfection and incompleteness on the planet from the time of Adam onward. Shortcomings, errors, ignorances, sins have been rife and have played their evil part at every stage of man's journey. The goal, the end, the purpose of man's spiritual creation has not yet taken visible shape and the hour is not come for God a second time to rest from His labours.

But humanity is not at a standstill. Humanity is on the move. As in distant ages material evolution swept forward in ordered triumph till at length it achieved its crowning work in man, so thereafter has spiritual evolution been sweeping irresistibly forward all the world over to achieve its purpose of developing a regenerate race of men who shall indeed be as children of God.

Man from the beginning is made in the likeness of God and his essential manhood never changes. But this likeness at first is rudimentary. It is no more than an embryo.

Only as the tree with its spreading boughs and its leaves is to be found in the seed from which it springs, is God's image to be found in the heart of the natural man. That heavenly image, before it can realise itself, needs to unfold and grow, and man's own will is assigned its share in that task of development. Not until that growth of the inward spiritual life is complete and until the fullness of its power has been reached, is man worthy of the name of man.

The New Testament, to emphasise the two moments of crisis in the spiritual growth of man, uses the striking figure of a twofold birth. Man is created as on the Sixth Day, the fine flower of material evolution endowed already with divine potentialities. He is born the natural man. When his latent powers are developed and he becomes equipped for a larger life, he enters the higher realm of the divine world—he is born anew, becomes a new creature, the spiritual man.

The human race passes through a development analogous to that of the individual. It is born in one state; and before it can come to its own it must be born again into another state. It is created in a condition of spiritual weakness and imperfection, and it must pass toilsomely through many stages of development before it can know its powers and achieve its destiny. The New Jerusalem is the figure under which the Second Birth of humanity is spoken of. A great part of the Apocalypse tells of the dreadful period of world-travail that precedes that birth. And those glorious passages which close our Bible, unparalleled for ecstasy and beauty in all our literature, are an effort to depict the exaltation and the wonder and the rapture and the joy and the everlasting blessedness that await the nations and the peoples of the earth when through the gates of spiritual attainment they enter into the presence of their Father and of the Lamb.

World-history has no other dénouement than this of the final Self-Revelation of God to His creatures. All events lead up to this and find their meaning in this, and apart from this they have no abiding value and lead to no abiding result. This is—so teaches the Bible—the supreme originating thought involved in creation, and it informs the whole creational process throughout.

CHAPTER III

MAN'S DESTINY AND MAN'S EFFORT

The spiritual evolution of man's soul is in this different from the evolution of his body, that it is not automatic nor unconscious, but demands from him directed effort. If he would advance, he must add his willing co-operation to that evolutionary urge which impels him on his upward way.

Spiritual life, both in the case of men and of nations, is likened by Jesus and others in the New Testament to a growing seed. The comparison for ever repudiates any idea of rigidity, fixity, immobility or stationariness in religion; but its positive meaning cannot be that man's mental progress is, like that of a plant, involuntary and effortless (men know otherwise); rather it is that man's spiritual nature is a living, growing thing which develops in an orderly manner continuously till it reaches fruition.

Jesus stated that 'the kingdom of God is within you', and likened its increase to that of a tiny 'mustard seed' which grows into a tree so big that birds sit in its branches —a comparison which illuminates the advance of spiritual knowledge both in the individual soul and in the soul of the human race.

More than once He compared spiritual truth to a seed which is sown in the heart of man and which grows according to the nature of the soil in which it falls. Truth and the human heart are by nature akin, and in a pure heart truth will grow apace and bring forth fruit abundantly; only some impurity and defect in the soil (such as worldly distractions or love of mammon) can prevent its growth.

The Baptist, emphasising this same process of spiritual growth in a larger field, compared the course of the Mosaic Dispensation to the growth of a crop of corn; when the allotted time had passed and the season of spiritual fruits had come, Jesus was sent with the power and authority of God to gather in the harvest of souls. As the Mosaic Dispensation passed away to be followed by another and a greater Dispensation, the Baptist warned the people of his time that though they might not know what was happening this was their Day of Judgment, and there was one among them gathering the fruits of Mosaism whether good or bad, a Divine Reaper 'Whose fan *is* in his hand, and he will throughly purge his floor, and gather his wheat into the garner; but he will burn up the chaff with unquenchable fire'. (Matt. iii. 12.)

In this simple but conclusive figure the Baptist taught that the Era of Moses was a set period in an evolutionary process, not unlike the allegorical 'day' in the account of material creation. Mosaism had its sowing, its time of maturing, and in the end its hour of reaping. The same evolutionary process was then begun again and carried forward a stage further by another Master. Jesus used (on more occasions than one) exactly the same figure with reference to His own Dispensation as John had used in referring to that of Moses. He likened it to good seed which He had sown in men's hearts but which was mixed by the evil one with tares; and the two would grow together to maturity till in the fullness of time the season of harvest came round: then God would send His angels and they would reap the whole field, which was the wide world, and would cast away and burn what was waste and worthless and would gather the righteous and true-hearted into the treasure-house of God.

Again the Baptist likens a Dispensation to a tree which, having increased to full size and borne its fruit and cast a seed from which another like tree may spring, is cut down to give room to a younger growth.

In the great allegory of the world-consummation of man's evolution given in Rev. xxii. 2, the Tree of Life is described as having attained the fullness of a universal fruitage, bearing twelve manner of fruits and yielding these every month, and as shedding from its leaves healing over all the nations of the wide earth.

But the need of moral effort is stressed in Scripture even more than the thought of growth. For practical results, man's special duty is to make a well-directed effort: if he does this, spiritual growth will follow of itself. Old Testament and New echo with exhortations from prophets and teachers calling men to abandon ease and negligence and gird themselves for endeavour—'seek', 'strive', 'labour on', 'quit you like men, be strong and of a good courage', 'fight the good fight, lay hold on eternal life', 'be instant in season and out of season', 'be ye doers of the word and not hearers only', 'in your patience ye shall win your souls', 'he that endureth to the end shall be saved'.

God must be sought if He is to be found; the truth must be striven for if it is to be realised.

If 'thou shalt seek the Lord thy God,' said Moses, 'thou shalt find *him*, if thou seek him with all thy heart and with all thy soul.' (Deut. iv. 29.)

'Ask, and it shall be given you,' said Christ; 'seek, and ye shall find; knock, and it shall be opened unto you . . . Strive to enter in at the strait gate: for many, I say unto you, will seek to enter in, and shall not be able.' (Matt. vii. 7 and Luke xiii. 24.)

Results are proportionate to the effort made.

God 'will render to every man according to his deeds,' for 'he is a rewarder of them that . . . seek him.' (Rom. ii. 6; Heb. xi. 6.)

This giving of battle, this seeking and striving, this patience and endurance takes in practical life many shapes and brings man face to face with many different problems. The Bible offers in the course of its narrative illustrations of a thousand diverse demands that duty may make on men. It gives particular and exact advice in many special cases. But whatever the circumstances may be and whether the emergency be great or small, the purpose and the essence of the effort that is required remain the same.

The object of all this struggle and endeavour is to draw out those high powers which lie folded away and hidden within the soul of every man as a rose is folded within the bud; to let the Divine Image in man's heart shine forth in its splendour; to become (so far as a human being may) godlike; and thus to co-operate with the evolutionary Force, with the spiritual impulse imparted to mankind by God.

That Heavenly Image is no material likeness; it occupies no space. It is a reflection of God as God is revealed to man; it is a reflection of those properties which are what we know of God, such as love, compassion, kindness, generosity, mercy, pity, faithfulness. These in their sum comprise our vision of God, and they are the elements which make up the Image graven in the human heart. The aim of man's effort is to bring these attributes into action, to use and exercise them, to give them strength and lead them on towards maturity. By doing deeds of goodness, by meditating on the perfections of God and holding communion with Him, man is enabled by degrees to develop divine characteristics and to become in a measure godlike. Thus he fulfils his possibilities and reaches up to his full moral stature.

The attributes of the Most High are the originals of the moral virtues for which Christ commanded men to strive. It is from this fact the virtues derive their authority and their eternal values. By cultivating them man makes himself like God. Christ said, 'Be ye perfect even as your Father in heaven is perfect', and there is no means of achieving this except by walking in the strait way of righteousness. Christ said, 'Come unto me', and no one can accept this invitation except by acquiring the divine attributes, for Christ was the express image of the Father and all the perfections of God in their fullness were manifest in Him.

The obligation to obey the injunctions of Christ, to be kind, generous, forgiving, compassionate, devoid of prejudice or partiality, peaceable, is not something imposed by a ruler's decree or an external power; it proceeds from man's own nature. The constitution of man's spiritual being imposes upon him the strict demands of duty. He is morally responsible before God, but he is also morally responsible to himself. He is compelled in the end to be his own judge. The strict and authoritative commands which Christ gave were given in the name of God Himself; but they were given, too, in the name of man's own heart. The laws of righteousness which He taught were the laws of man's own being, and the godliness which He bade men develop was already as a potentiality laid up within them, 'hidden that it might be revealed'.

The divine image in man is part of himself, it is indeed his true self, the essence of his existence, the soul of his soul. In purifying his heart that this likeness may shine forth in its beauty and in its truth, he is not only drawing near to God but is also becoming himself, is finding himself: he passes out of spiritual weakness and infancy into maturity. His faculties and endowments, aided by the law of growth, establish among themselves a balance and symmetry and order; he is happy and wins that rest unto his soul which Christ promised to those who came to Him. If through neglect he does not cause the heavenly qualities within to expand, the loss is his. He stunts himself, he limits himself; he chooses infirmity instead of power.

The combination of faith and works on which the New Testament so vigorously insists is not a strange or arbitrary demand. Good deeds in fact spring from those heavenly attributes—those promptings to kindness and compassion—which God's love has planted in the human heart: were it not for that inborn goodness no man could be moved to a good deed. But without faith he cannot know what those attributes are, nor whence they come nor what they mean nor whither they lead. Man cannot by reason alone know what God is like; and since he cannot know what God is like he cannot by reason alone know himself—since he is made in the image of God. For true self-knowledge, self-understanding, faith is needed as well as reason. Without faith man cannot comprehend the nature of moral principle nor its foundations; he cannot appreciate the force of its imperatives nor the extent of its rewards and its punishments. Without faith he cannot be moved by the highest and most exalting of all motives, love of God for God's own sake.

As the development of God's attributes produces within the soul harmony and order and peace, so it produces harmony, order and peace in the community. The divine virtues are the cement of society. Without them the disruptive influence of human passions and of the struggle for existence cannot be kept in check. Qualities such as unselfishness, pity, kindness, fidelity, forbearance, forgiveness develop a sense of solidarity and establish concord. Under their influence men become ever more ready to relieve, to help and to uplift one another and labour with increasing earnestness to build a social order in which even justice shall be done, wrongs shall be redressed and the spirit of fraternity shall become the rule of life. Compassion and goodwill create an environment which itself aids their own further growth. And since these high qualities descend to earth from heaven and come from a God who pours forth His love universally on all mankind alike and sends His sunshine and His rain on the just and the unjust, therefore their unifying power will never be exhausted nor reach an end till they have spread out and embraced the whole world. Compassion and goodwill among men, if they be a true image of their originals in God, will know no partiality nor any bound or limit; they will reach everywhere regardless of all barriers.

God is for ever one. His attributes do not change; for from the beginning they are perfect and any change would be towards imperfection. He is eternally the same. There is for all members of the human race one ultimate spiritual ideal. All men come forth from the one God; and to the one God all must return. When Christ said 'Be ye perfect as your Father in heaven', He made the same one Being to be the common ideal of all men, and held up the same Spiritual Perfection to be the object of all men's aspiration and the goal of all men's effort.

Christ proposed the recognition of God's oneness as the centre, the harmonising force of world unity. He brought to its clearest definition a system of thought which is implied throughout Scripture. He gathered the whole of human life around the throne of God. He based —as Moses and the Law and the prophets had done before him—civilisation on ethics, ethics on spirituality, spirituality on the effort to develop those godlike properties which God made to be the very self of the human soul. Happiness, order, peace, progress, all are to be the result of spiritual growth and moral effort. Any scheme of social amelioration or national advancement which neglects divine law and leaves aside faith and righteousness must lead to disappointment. This is the basis of that sublime practical truth to which the great teachers of the Bible so often and so vainly bear witness, that in spite of appearances, in spite of illusions which tempt and deceive, success and prosperity cannot be gained in any high degree nor maintained for any length of time except when in alignment with the divine purpose. On the contrary, since God's mercy and forbearance though great are not without limit, any attempt to traverse or thwart God's will must bring spiritual retribution and will assuredly involve a guilty nation in disappointment and disaster.

The language of the prophets is not our language and

their point of view is not that of the modern world. But it is not difficult to see that their counsels and warnings have a scientific and logical aspect, and express principles of divine government which are as active today as they were in the days of the Jewish kings. In the Book of Isaiah it is written,

> If ye be willing and obedient, ye shall eat the good of the land: But if ye refuse and rebel, ye shall be devoured with the sword: for the mouth of the Lord hath spoken *it*. (Isa. i. 19–20.)

And again:

> Woe to them that go down to Egypt for help; and stay on horses, and trust in chariots, because *they are* many; and in horsemen, because they are very strong; but they look not unto the Holy One of Israel, neither seek the Lord! (Isa. xxxi. 1.)

Or again:

> . . . thou hast trusted in thy wickedness: thou hast said, None seeth me. Thy wisdom and thy knowledge, it hath perverted thee; and thou hast said in thine heart, I *am*, and none else beside me. Therefore shall evil come upon thee; thou shalt not know from whence it riseth: and mischief shall fall upon thee; thou shalt not be able to put it off: and desolation shall come upon thee suddenly, *which* thou shalt not know. (Isa. xlvii. 10–11.)

Long before Isaiah, Moses had declared to the Israelites the same truth and had given a warning (which they did not heed):

> . . . thou shalt remember the Lord thy God: for *it is* he that giveth thee power to get wealth, that he may establish his covenant which he sware unto thy fathers, as *it is* this day. And it shall be, if thou do at all forget the Lord thy God, and walk after other gods, and serve them, and worship them, I testify against you this day that ye shall surely perish. (Deut. viii. 18–19.)

And long after Isaiah Jesus summarised the principle in His pronouncement: 'Seek ye first the kingdom of God, and his righteousness; and all these things shall be added unto you.'

The whole Bible gives voice to God's demand from man of this increasing spiritual effort, but no one else sets the demand so high nor insists upon it with such sternness as the Lord Christ. Every other effort, He urges, and every other aim is to be subordinated to this. Every other loyalty is to be postponed to it. None is to allow any danger to deter him nor any difficulty to discourage him. If need be, pain, persecution, shame and even death must be faced: at any cost, the effort to walk in God's way and to follow after righteousness must be maintained. No other effort is so richly rewarded; and neglect of this effort brings its own dire retribution.

So Jesus spoke. And in the light of that law of spiritual evolution which in this age we begin to understand we are able to appreciate the wisdom and the pity which prompted His commands and His warnings.

CHAPTER IV

THE OVERLORD OF EVOLUTION

But if a man's volition plays a part in his spiritual growth and he is required to participate in his own evolution, he remains always in the position of a servant and a dependent. His responsibility, while strictly enforced, is limited. His power lies wholly within a narrow range. It is not his own through any dignity or original right of his: it is freely conferred on him by the Creator who had He pleased might have withheld it, as He withheld it from lower realms of creation—from plants and planets. Man did not by his superiority wrest any share of the evolutionary power from God and use it according to his own human desire. What he has, God gave him, and God having entrusted him with this power insists that he use it aright.

Discussing spiritual evolution in its largeness, the Bible proves that the part of man is humble in the extreme, and that nothing is so likely to stultify and disable him, to bring him to failure and unhappiness, as the delusion that he is an independent agent and can take the laws of life and progress into his own hands.

Throughout the Bible God stands for ever supreme, and man never is (nor ever can be) more than His creature and His servant. Man's ignorance of this truth and his revolt against it are the signs of his immaturity and the causes of his frustrations. As he reaches the height of his powers he becomes more and more humble and submissive, and attains increasing power and happiness through an ever-growing efficiency in service.

It is not in the power of the race to originate the idea of its evolution, to design the path along which this evolution will proceed, the end to which it will lead or the forces that will start the process and keep it in movement till the predetermined end is reached.

Nor is an individual any more able to create his own power to grow, or able to arrange for the method or the goal of his growth. In this respect he is no more free than is the seed of corn to which Christ compared him. The seed's growth is an orderly process, first the blade then the ear, then the full corn in the ear; and spiritual growth is in like manner according to an imposed and inviolable law.

The law under which his spiritual development is directed and the purpose to which it points are made by Another Mind than his. The force on which he draws continually and by dint of which alone he moves is derived from a Greater Will than his.

He is for ever in a position of complete dependence, the child of a hidden and everlasting power, the subject of a law which he cannot question nor change. He may take all he has and is for granted and live in a dream-house of illusion; but no amount of ignorance or self-will can alter the fact or the degree of his servitude. There is no way of deliverance for him from that great movement into which he was born and within the control of which he must eternally remain.

Because God is supreme and man's whole duty is to serve Him, the Bible represents that man's proper approach to truth and life, to all knowledge and all action, is through religion. It sets forth evolution in its religious aspect. Any enquiry after truth which begins by separating man from God is wrong from the first, is the essence of falsity. The notion that man is independent, that he has the prerogative of laying out the paths of history and of civilisation, the privilege of doing whatever seems best to his own will and his own desire is born of arrogance and is utter illusion.

Evolution indeed from its beginning in the distant past to its completion in the distant future is nothing more than the Revelation of God's purpose for mankind. What is being evolved was first created by God, then infolded by God, then unfolded to man's knowledge by God: the plan, the process and the substance of the process are all from God. The story of the spiritual evolution of man from his infancy to his maturity, from Genesis to the close of the Apocalypse, is the story of the continuous progressive Self-Revelation of God to man. The first creation of man, when God engraves within the being of His creature His Own Image, is itself a high act of Self-Revelation; and the whole movement of evolution that follows is in every part and aspect a manifesting of the unity of God, of the completeness of His dominion, the perfection of His love, the beauty, the glory and the beneficence of His everlasting and inviolable Purpose for mankind.

Man's part therein is not of his own making. It is permitted only. He is at best a servant. God's command precedes all man's activity, and all that man in any circumstances can do is either to obey or to disobey—he does not really initiate or originate anything: all the beginnings are with God.

Man's ability, too, to co-operate in his own evolution depends on the extent and the accuracy of his knowledge of God, and the measure of his knowledge is the measure of his progress towards spiritual maturity.

The Bible, therefore, as a practical guide-book to man in his evolutionary journey extols in the most impressive images, in the strongest language, and with the utmost earnestness the eternal and unqualified supremacy of God. Its first counsel and its last is that men shall trust God, shall study His law and obey His will. The worst mistake possible for man to make is to pass out from under the law of God and commit his future to the misguidance of his own phantasmal imagination.

God is revealed as One, Eternal and Infinite, unchanging, pervading and sustaining all existence. His throne rests upon equity and justice; the heavens declare His greatness and all the nations behold His majesty, but He Himself is hidden from man's face in clouds and darkness, and remains above the reach of human knowledge.

The whole earth and its peoples are subject to Him and none can stand against His might or question His authority.

> . . . beside me there is no God.
>
> Turn to me and you are saved, all ends of the earth! As I am God and God alone, I swear by myself . . . that every knee shall bow to me, and every tongue swear loyalty. (Isa. xlv. 22–23.)
>
> . . . the rules of my religion I send forth to light up every nation. (Isa. li. 4.) I now appoint you to bring light to the nations, that my salvation may reach the world's end. (Isa. xlix. 6.)

> Woe to the man who quarrels with his Maker—man a mere potsherd of the earth! Does the clay ask the potter what he is doing? does what he makes tell him he is powerless? . . . And would you question me about the future? Would you dictate to me about my work? (Isa. xlv. 9, 11.)

Again and again God asserts He has His plan for mankind both in large and in little, and that none can frustrate His purpose nor bend Him from His determination.

> As I have planned, so shall it stand, as I have purposed, so shall it be . . . So is it in my purpose for the world, so I stretched out my arm against all nations. The Eternal's purpose who can disannul? His outstretched arm, who turns it back? (Isa. xiv. 24, 26, 27.)
>
> From of old I am God, and from henceforth the same; no one can snatch out of my hand, and what I do none can reverse. (Isa. xliii. 13.)

He foresees and fore-ordains the developments of history and according to His pleasure foretells the same to His prophets and to mankind.

> I am God and there is none like me, I who foretell the end from the beginning, and from of old what is to be, saying, 'My purpose shall stand, I carry out whate'er I choose . . . I have said it, I will do it, I will carry out my plan.' (Isa. xlvi. 9–11.)

It is He Who raises up nations and empires, Who

guides and protects them, and if they prove unworthy abases them at a time and in a manner decreed by Him.

It is He Who summons a Prophet (Isa. vi. 8–9) and (Jer. i. 5 and 10) even appoints him before he is born into the world:

> Before I formed you in the womb, I chose you; ere ever you were born, I set you apart; I have appointed you a prophet to the nations . . . here and now I give you authority over nations and kingdoms, to tear up, to break down, to shatter, to pull down, to build up and to plant.

He loves righteousness, justice, mercy and for these gives nations and men rich rewards. But He hates evil, oppression, unfaithfulness and hypocrisy, and for these things and such as these He brings on men condign punishment:

> Ah . . . sinful nation, . . . Why will you earn fresh strokes, for holding on in your revolt? . . . (Isa. i. 4–5.)

He is not satisfied with the pretence of loyalty and devotion.

> Your sacred festivals? I hate them, scorn them; . . . you offer me your gifts? I will not take them; . . . No more of your hymns for me! I will not listen to your lutes. No, let justice well up like fresh water, let honesty roll in full tide . . . (Amos v. 21–24.)

> . . . I instruct them by my words, this precept shines out plain: love I desire, not sacrifice, knowledge of God, not any offering. (Hos. vi. 5–6.)

He 'reveals His inner mind to man' and man must meet Him in frankness and sincerity.

Knowing the future and loving His creatures He warns men beforehand of coming retribution that they may avoid it.

> Listen—it is the Eternal speaking—be not too proud to hearken; do honour to the Eternal, to your God, before the darkness falls, before your footsteps stumble on the twilight hills, before the gleam you look for turns to a dead gloom. If you will not listen, then I must weep in secret for your pride, mine eyes must stream with tears, for the Eternal's flock borne off to exile . . . (Jer. xiii. 15–17.)

For God, though He will not condone disobedience, is 'full of compassion and gracious, slow to anger . . .' (Ps. lxxxvi. 15.) He is a shield to His people, their refuge and help in trouble; He is their shepherd, the mother bird guarding its young, the Host and Friend of the faithful, the Father of the fatherless. (Ps. lxviii. 5.)

For all His transcendence He dwells with the poor and lowly.

> I sit on high, enthroned, the Majestic One, and I am with the crushed and humbled soul, to revive the spirit of the humble, and to put heart into the crushed. (Isa. lvii. 15.)

His last word in dealing with His creatures is always of mercy and forgiveness:

> . . . he pardons all your sins, and all your sicknesses he heals, he saves your life from death, he crowns you with his love and pity. . . (Ps. ciii. 3–4.)

And though His prophets in fierce and terrible language announce the fierceness and the terror of God's vengeance, yet with one voice they all predict that at the end when His people's guilt is purged God's bounty will bestow an ultimate and final restoration.

The witness of the New Testament to God's greatness, though the same in spirit, is even more intimate and full than that of the Old. God's consciousness encloses all existence and He does not withhold Himself at any time from anything that He has made. The least-regarded objects of nature, the lonely flower of the mountain-side, the raven, the despised sparrow, all receive His bounty and are under His care in their life and in their death. He watches over every human being, making provision for his needs and numbering even the very hairs of his head. Nothing escapes His knowledge; nothing is too minute for His attention. He is the giver of health, the healer in sickness, the remover of disabilities. So closely does He identify Himself with men that whatever men do to one another for good or ill is recorded in heaven as though done to Him. The most casual, the most trifling deed of kindness to a believer is never unremembered nor unrewarded by God. On Him man depends not only for his daily sustenance and his physical well-being, but for his moral and spiritual growth; and for the energy of his intellectual life. The mental powers of man, and even his freedom of will, are subject to the good pleasure of God. It is He Who opens or closes the ears of men to the teaching of Christ, and none can come to Christ except through the initiative and the bidding of the Father. He knows what is in man and reads the unuttered thoughts of the individual and foresees the individual's future acts even though these be quite unknown and incredible to the individual himself. He foresees the changes of history, the wars and tumults of nations in the far future, and likewise the great convulsions or the frustrations of natural processes—the earthquakes, the famines and the like—that lie in wait for humanity.

Not in this earth-life only, but in the worlds that lie beyond the grave, it rests with God to determine the lot and destiny of His creatures. No constraint is put upon Him. No other will than His own determines His decision. No other opinion is weighed or taken. To God alone it belongs to punish men or to reward them. He has established the law of justice as the law of the universe, and from His judgment there is here or hereafter no escape and no appeal. Men may kill the body, but there the power permitted to them ends. God can admit to heaven or cast into hell. He is indeed the all-terrible. He is truly to be feared—He, and no other. And whoever has learned to fear God becomes thereby immune from every other fear.

To command and to create are the prerogatives of God. There is none to share these with Him. Man through the very nature of his existence is altogether the creature of God, and no course ever is or can be open to him save that of service to his Lord. Even if this service were (what it cannot be) utterly perfect—even if it were never for a moment qualified, if there were no hesitancy or error or incompleteness in it, it would then only meet the requirements of justice and fulfil the bare demands of duty.

In an age when the idea of progress was unfamiliar or unknown, when reverence for law was not what it has now become and when the exercise of arbitrary power was regarded as the prerogative and proof of kingship, Christ revealed quite clearly the evolving purpose of God, so that in His light we can see it throughout the Bible moving by an orderly process regularly and irresistibly forward through millenniums. God designed, decreed and executed as He saw fit, but always according to a principle of justice which evolution not only enforces on mankind, but also embodies in its own operation. The whole life of the race and of every member thereof from the dawn of human history to its dusk, lies within the scope of this vast Progress. The onward drive of the purpose of God is irresistible. Evil lifts its head in ignorant rebellion, but if they who seek their own ends, not God's, rally to its banner they can but stunt their own growth and are left at last to wail and gnash their teeth upon themselves for the opportunity which they have forfeited and which can never come again.

For all his freedom man cannot check the development of God's purpose nor hide himself from the foreknowledge of the Ancient of Days. That spiritual evolution of humanity which is slowly taking shape among the peoples of the earth is in truth mysteriously the manifestation in time and in space of realities previously hidden in eternity, already created and already existent in heaven in the mind of God.

The events of history are not a series of haphazards or

impromptus in which God meets emergencies as they arise. The power which carries evolution through to its preordained end is the power which in the beginning created man. It knows neither fluctuation nor limitation; it is altogether independent and all sufficient; and in spite of human rebellion it effects in its own way and its own time a purpose laid down before the foundation of the world.

CHAPTER V

THE MINISTERS OF EVOLUTION

The Bible reveals that the creation of the material world was carried through by stages, in a series of separate periods each complete in itself and each following the same pattern.

> And God said . . . And the evening and the morning were the first day.
>
> And God said . . . And the evening and the morning were the second day.

And finally:

> And God said . . . And the evening and the morning were the sixth day.

The spiritual evolution of man from his First Birth in Genesis to his Second Birth in the Apocalypse is revealed as being likewise carried through by stages, in a series of separate periods, each complete in itself and each following the same pattern.

The Bible does not state what is meant by the word 'Day', beyond a clear indication that it had not a literal but a symbolic meaning; for the sun which makes the material day was not created till the fourth of these periods. But it gives a clear account of the division of the evolutionary movement into great Eras, all having certain characteristics the same and having definite epochs and moments of crisis. These Eras are generally known as Dispensations, but they are sometimes spoken of in Scripture by the same name as the Days of creation. 'Your father Abraham rejoiced to see my day,' said Jesus, referring to His Dispensation. And the time of the end, the time when all things are made new and the Father and the Lamb come to dwell among men is often called the Day of the Lord, meaning the Day when Christ shall reign in the Glory of the Lord God.

The comparison of Christ's Dispensation to a Day is evidently appropriate because He likened Himself to the sun. 'I am the light of the world,' He said. Everything was, save for His illumination, in darkness; and those who believed in Him became children of the light, able to reflect on others the light they gained from Him, their Sun.

The time of the Second Advent is, for the same reason, fitly likened to a Day, for the Father and the Son give it light. 'The city had no need of the sun.' Besides the Dispensation of Christ and that which is to follow His Second Advent in the power of the Father, there are definitely referred to in Scripture three other Dispensations. One is that of Moses, which is narrated from its beginning to its close. Another is that of Abraham, the Father of the Faithful, which is briefly and distinctly sketched. The third is that of Noah. Christ compared the phenomena of Noah's Advent to those which would occur at the future time of His own Second Advent: 'As it was in the days of Noe.'

As the people of the world had disregarded Christ at His first coming in Bethlehem, so had they disregarded Noah long ages before, and so would they disregard the coming of the Son of Man in the clouds of heaven, and would be oblivious of everything except their own mundane pursuits.

Each Dispensation opened a New Covenant between God and man; each covered a term of years and was succeeded by another Dispensation. Each was inaugurated by a Master Spirit, a man who was specially called by the Most High to the task, and who after his death, continued to be the supreme sole guide and governor of his people so long as the Dispensation endured.

Of the four Supreme Mediators named in Scripture, three are connected especially with Palestine and all arose in the East.

It would seem as if God not only ordained certain Great Souls to play the lead in the drama of evolution, and arranged the times of their manifestation and occultation, but that He also designated certain lands for certain purposes. He appoints not only the time of the Prophet's birth, but its place also, and the place where his prophetic work is to be done.

Palestine has been a holy land for some four thousand years not to Jews and Christians only but to Muslims also. Its holiness does not attach to the inhabitants. The people who dwell in it are not holy: the Jews were called by the Baptist a generation of vipers. The land itself, the Land of Promise, is holy, because it is associated with the life and the labour of so many of God's Holiest Ones, and because it was selected by Him to be the scene of so important a phase in the spiritual evolution of mankind.

If Palestine occupies throughout the Bible a central place, the whole progress of redemption (back to mythic days and forward to times visible only in prophecy) is shown as belonging to the East, to the one continent of Asia. Europe and Africa come into the record: Egypt in especial seems to be a region of privilege, for not only the Hebrew people but the three outstanding figures of the Bible, Abraham, Moses and Christ, were all sojourners there, and attention is drawn in the Gospel to the prophecy 'Out of Egypt have I called my son'. (Matt. ii. 15.) The West as a vast tract is likewise mentioned. But Europe, Africa and the West take a secondary position as recipients of a spiritual illumination which first arises in the Orient. The Second Coming itself (like earlier Advents) is expressly compared by Christ to the lightning which 'cometh out of the east . . . and shineth even unto the west'. (Matt. xxiv. 27.)

World-history outside the borders of the Bible testifies, as many have observed, to the same fact, and seems to corroborate the Bible principle of the primacy of the East in the origination of spiritual teaching. No world-prophet has ever arisen except in Asia. There is no world-religion extant which was not first proclaimed in Asia. There is nothing recognised as a Holy Scripture which did not make its appearance in Asia. Whatever contribution the Western world may have made to human progress and spiritual evolution, it has not contributed a Scripture, a Religion or the Founder of a Religion.

As God chooses for a particular reason this land or that according to His wisdom and man may not alter or modify the divine decision, so, too, with the great epochs and crises of the evolutionary process. It is for God the Father to determine times and seasons. Man cannot choose the dates when Dispensations begin or end, nor by his own knowledge or calculation discover what these dates shall be. Joseph, who through his saintliness was in touch with the eternal plane, foretold the appearance of Moses: '. . . God will surely visit you, and bring you out of this land unto . . .' (Gen. l. 24.) But he could not indicate name or date. Moses foretold the Advent of his Successor but made no suggestion as to the time of His coming. The Scribes and Pharisees with all their learning and parade of holiness were so far from having any idea as to when the Messiah would appear that they could not even recognise the time when it arrived; and the Jews are still looking forward to a date which is nearly two thousand years behind them. God ordains the times and seasons of history, but does not communicate them to men nor to angels; nor does Scripture give any guidance to men in this respect, nor open a way into the wisdom of God. The Dispensations of the Redemptive Scheme are not of the same nor of like length: that of Moses was twice as long as that of Abraham, and no clue is given in Scripture as to the reason for this difference. Epochs and Eras are ordered by God: man's part is to recognise the transitions when God brings them to pass.

On these whom God appoints as the Suns of the Days of Spiritual Creation, or Lords of Dispensations, He bestows spectacular power. They stand out in greatness above all other men. The two thousand two hundred years and more of Hebrew history narrated in the Bible are dominated by three heroic figures, and the earlier period of pre-Hebrew history is, in like manner, dominated by the earlier Covenant-bringer Noah. The Dispensations of these four Leaders are treated in a very unequal manner. The Age of Moses is sketched in its full length, and from its inauguration in Egypt to its close in the epoch of Jesus Christ. The four books of Exodus, Leviticus, Numbers and Deuteronomy are parallel to the four Gospels of Christ, Joshua to the Acts of the Apostles, the Prophets to the Epistles, and perhaps the Apocalypse of Daniel to the Apocalypse of John. But there is nothing in the New Testament to correspond to the historical books of Judges and Kings and Samuel and Chronicles and Ezra and Nehemiah. Only two generations are covered by the New Testament narrative, and the rest of Christian history is written elsewhere than in the canon of Scripture. But the Bible record shows that as Christ in His time overshadowed the peoples, so did Abraham and Noah likewise in their time. Each was supreme in his own Day over the people committed to him, and was remembered and venerated long ages after his Day had passed away. Of Moses, God said to Aaron: 'He shall be to thee as God.' Moses' essential superiority to any other seer or saint or prophet in his time is emphasised in God's rebuke to Miriam and Aaron. (Num. xii. 6–9.)

God spoke and said:

> Hear now my words: If there be a prophet among you, *I* the Lord will make myself known unto him in a vision, *and* will speak unto him in a dream. My servant Moses *is* not so, who *is* faithful in all mine house. With him will I speak mouth to mouth, even apparently, and not in dark speeches; and the similitude of the Lord shall he behold: wherefore then were ye not afraid to speak against my servant Moses? And the anger of the Lord was kindled against them . . .

Even Isaiah and his brother prophets did not equal

themselves with the Lord of their Era, nor do more than elucidate and apply the meanings of his Revelation.

Moses, prophesying the coming of the Messiah, compared his own status to that of Christ: 'The Lord thy God will raise up . . . a Prophet . . . like unto me . . .' (Deut. xviii. 15.) The same attribution of divine honour to Moses appears in prophecy at the close of the New Testament, when the Redeemed chanting in heaven the praise of God are thus described:

> And they sing the song of Moses, the servant of God, and the song of the Lamb, saying, Great and marvellous *are* thy works, Lord God Almighty . . . (Rev. xv. 3.)

Not until Christ did anyone arise to give a New Teaching instead of that of Moses and to take to Himself the authority which once had been Moses', as fifteen hundred years before Moses had taken the Torch of Revelation from Abraham. Day succeeds Day. Each Day has one Sun; and there is no light to challenge that of the sun.

But to the power even of the greatest of these prophets there is one definite limitation. Spiritual evolution does not move forward through any coercion of the wills of men. God requires that men of their own volition shall co-operate with Him. He does not substitute His will for their wills, nor does He, so to speak, drive their development onward by any output of main force. He educates and trains them little by little and measures His requirements to their growing strength of mind and heart. Those Supreme Prophets, therefore, who are His Agents and the Masters of Evolution, are limited by the capacity of the people. They cannot put a bushel of truth into a pint measure. They cannot teach more than their hearers can learn. The fact that Moses revealed only elementary religious truths does not prove that Moses knew no more, but that the people were unwilling and unable to receive more. The scope and range of his teachings, if we had an accurate record of them, would indicate the moral and spiritual condition of the twelve tribes at that time, but it would not suggest at all the extent of Moses' wisdom.

Jesus frequently lamented over the people's slowness of understanding, the feebleness of their faith; and this sorrow of His was not caused by any personal impatience, but by His sad knowledge that they thus forfeited many blessings and happinesses He might have bestowed upon them had they been worthy to receive them. It is written of Him once expressly, that 'He could there do no mighty work because of their unbelief', and on another occasion, when conversing with His disciples, towards the end of His life, He said, 'Other things I have to tell you but ye cannot bear them now.' In all the speeches and addresses of Moses and of Christ there is no sign of an overbearing attitude of mind nor of a desire to browbeat opposition or to startle or stun the imagination of their hearers. In spite of the power they exercised and the divine authority they claimed, both of these Mighty Ones were personally gentle and humble. Jesus was meek and lowly in heart. A disciple who knew and loved Him well described Him as one who 'when he was reviled, reviled not again; when he suffered, he threatened not . . .' (I Peter ii. 23.) And of Moses it is written: 'Now the man Moses *was* very meek, above all the men which *were* upon the face of the earth'. (Num. xii. 3.)

With scrupulous care Jesus respected the personal independence of everyone He addressed. He gave everybody full liberty of choice, even when by this He was Himself involved in danger. He knew well that Judas would betray Him; yet Judas was a man of great spiritual possibilities, and Jesus gave him every opportunity, admitting him to the intimacies of discipleship and treating him with every kindness to the end: the use that Judas made of the privileges was an act of his own unfettered will for which the responsibility was entirely his own.

The simplicity and quietness with which Jesus appeared among men, like that of Moses' appearance long before, was due to the demands of the same great principle. Had His Advent been accompanied by signs and wonders on a great scale, the faith and sincerity of the people would not have been tested. There would have been no room for freedom of choice. Men's minds would have been appalled; their judgment dethroned; their imagination enslaved; their wills coerced to accept and to submit to an evident proof of superhuman power. Every human being (good, bad and indifferent alike), Caiaphas, Herod, Pilate, the Scribes, the Pharisees, the fickle mob, the Gentiles, along with Peter and James and John, would all have been reduced to a common level of moral surrender and of compelled subjection to the New Revelation. Whereas, to recognise a Lord of the Ages in a humble artisan from Galilee, or a young shepherd from the mountains of Midian, would be a proof of intuitive vision and sincerity of heart. Through this freedom of choice, the Cause of God has brought among men division, combat and confusion. No man can refuse or escape from the responsibility of decision: he must be on one side or the other, with God's Cause or against it. Whichever side he espouses, the choice is his own. God does not coerce him to join the army of light nor yet prevent him from joining the army of darkness. If we read of Pharaoh that God hardened his heart, that is to say, God could have softened it but did not: God permitted Pharaoh to make his own choice.

Men are judged by God according to the attitude they adopt to His Cause. If they choose to forward it, Christ compares them to white-fleeced sheep, calls them His children or children of light, and pronounces blessings on them. If they oppose it, He likens them to black-fleeced goats, and warns them that darkness and retribution will be their lot.

Social classifications made on the ground of wealth, rank, learning, appearance, reputation and the like, such as the world uses, are in the Bible regarded as of small importance. The true basis for division is spirituality. There are in God's eyes two kinds of men only—the spiritual and the unspiritual. Between these two groups an internecine struggle is waged for ever. One unceasing relentless battle continues down the ages without intermission. The participants change with the generations: the battle changes not. Abel, Isaac, Jacob, Joseph, Joshua, Elijah, Nathan, David, Job, Isaiah and Amos, Rachel and Hannah and Huldah, and Peter and Paul and Mary Magdalene: and over against them, Cain and Pharaoh and Agag and Ahaz and Ahab and Jezebel and Ahaziah and Herod and Pilate and Judas and Caiaphas—always, in every age, there are men and women to be found who, of their own choice, range themselves on either side to carry on the everlasting conflict. And though the members of each army seem a strangely mixed and highly heterogeneous company, yet they are regarded by God as all alike either in eternal glory or eternal shame.

The Kingdom of God is not shown in Scripture as progressing in its own strength or pursuing in history a smooth and even course. Its chief supporters are not always the mighty and the great, the cultivated and the learned. The Divine Cause moves forward through tumult and uproar, through bitter struggles and discouragement and defeat and recovery and indefatigable perseverance. Its advance is secured through the aid of brave and earnest human souls, through the efforts of men and women (most of them poor, obscure, unknown), who in their hearts faithfully accept the decree of the Beloved, and submitting to his good pleasure with deeper and ever deeper humility, contend steadfastly against their own self-will and the misdirected wills of those who, through self-love, would thwart the unfolding purpose of the Creator. From Genesis to Revelation, the Bible is a moving picture of this great battle. The issue hangs always in the balance. There is never a definite decision, a conclusive victory. Again and again Truth and Righteousness are worsted. The combat grows fiercer with the centuries, and evil in the New Testament seems to win its extremest victory. John the Baptist, 'a prophet and more than a prophet' is beheaded; Jesus Christ, the most glorious Figure of all, the beloved Son of God, is Himself brought to destruction and crucified. Even the apostles sink for a moment into despair.

Such are in history the fruits of man's free-will. Such are the results of the respect which God's Messengers pay to the independent volition of men. Because men are free, therefore in the world the Kingdom of God is neglected, ridiculed, scorned, opposed, perverted. Because men are free, God's Holy Ones are assailed and martyred.

But though the High Prophets, such as Jesus or Moses, thus withhold the use of personal force or any form of compulsion; though they, themselves, submit to violence and wrong and show forbearance and gentleness under every provocation, yet they have a reserve of power which enables them to accomplish fully the work committed to them by God. They cannot be resisted. In spite of every difficulty, in spite of the unworthiness of the world, in spite of the incapacity, the vacillation, the faithlessness of the people, they do not fail. They are the Lords, the Divine Agents of the Spiritual Evolution of the race; and this Evolution is an integral system ordained by the Almighty. The power of the whole is behind its every phase, its every movement. Ignorant and foolish men can bring about their own undoing; they cannot frustrate the purpose of God. Every Dispensation is charged with ample power to fulfil its part and function in the grand Creative Scheme of God. And the Bible reaches its stupendous climax when Jesus Christ announces that the triumphant conclusion of that Scheme is now near at hand, and when St. John's apocalypse unveils in prophetic narrative a celestial picture of the victories of God and the exaltation of righteousness and justice to the throne of the world.

CHAPTER VI

THE POWER OF CHRIST

The world which Jesus was to master and to make anew ignored Him in His lifetime. The one authentic account of His work is contained in the New Testament, and from its record we see that the power afterwards manifested in full measure made from the first an immediate impression on His contemporaries. It astonished and pleased the open-minded and the receptive; it alarmed the ecclesiastical authorities who feared it might supplant their own. It did not cease nor weaken with His death, but deepened and extended till it became the constructive principle in Western civilisation.

Jesus' possession of this power is the more remarkable because He was himself meek and lowly in heart, compassionate and loving; and the moral elevation which He produced among the nations is associated with the gentler virtues of pity and forgiveness, of charity and self-sacrifice. There is nothing in His environment to explain His extraordinary influence. It was not due to the qualities of His time and country, nor to the intellectual climate in which His human lot was cast. He did not owe it in any way to His compatriots; on the contrary, He exerted it in spite of their denial and opposition. Though in Him Hebrew tradition was lifted to world-wide eminence and glory, yet in His lifetime He was but an obscure member of a despised and down-trodden people; He had neither wealth nor social position nor any material advantage to use for the advance of His cause; His public career lasted less than three years and He confined His activities to the declaration of a purely spiritual truth.

From the beginning it was the singular power of Jesus' teaching which impressed those who heard Him. He had power over their minds and hearts, power over unclean spirits, power over even the winds and waves. The authority with which He spoke was quite new to them. (Matt. vii. 28–29.) It was altogether different from that of the Scribes, who would spin academic elaborations that had no penetrating or illuminating quality whatever. St. Matthew notes that 'the multitudes were astonished at his teaching: For he taught them as *one* having authority, and not as their scribes.' St. Luke comments, 'And they were astonished at his teaching; for his word was with authority,' and again, '. . . they spake together, one with another, saying, What is this word? for with authority and power he commandeth the unclean spirits, and they come out.' (Matt. vii. 28–29; Luke iv. 32, 36.) Whence this power came or what was its nature none could tell. All men felt it; but none could account for it. Some said it came from God, others that it came from Beelzebub, all agreed it was beyond their experience, beyond any earthly explanation. We who read in the Gospels the record of His spoken word, can ourselves still feel in His utterance something of the quality which astonished His contemporaries. If when spoken it was unlike the manner of the scribes, when written it is unlike that of poet or orator, and has a force and winningness altogether unique. There is no special beauty of form or of diction. His teaching—all of it, even the most illustrious and moving parts of it, the Sermon on the Mount, for instance, or the Parable of the Prodigal—is artless, spontaneous, conversational. There is no dogmatic assertive eloquence such as might overbear and carry away an audience. There is never a straining after effect, nor any desire to impress. He promised to those who learned of Him that they would find rest unto their souls; and we find that quality in the nature of His utterance. It breathes serenity, and radiates the calm of assurance and certain knowledge. When one contemplates any of the processes of the natural world, the coming of spring, the growing of the corn, the unfolding of the leaves, one marvels at so great a demonstration of power with so little an appearance of effort. So it is with the teaching of the Lord Jesus: His power seems almost effortless. All the generations have felt that power and they feel it still—a power poured resistlessly forth from illimitable reserves. But no saint, no poet, no philosopher, has ever produced the effect that He produced, or spoken as He spoke. No man can imitate that power nor set up a like power against it. It is incommunicable and above explanation. It is Jesus' own, and remained for ordinary men a secret and a mystery.

Not only did His friends, the open-minded and well-disposed, feel it. The Rabbis, too, felt it, and hated Him because of it. They quickly realised He had a power which they had not. They perceived at once that His challenge to their prerogative was formidable. His ministry had hardly begun when they resolved that this teaching could not be allowed to continue. This young man must be suppressed. It was envy pure and simple which aroused the opposition of the priests. It was envy which hardened them against Him, which induced them to seek to entrap Him, to conspire against His life. When by a dark intrigue, before He had been teaching three years, they compassed His death, the unjust judge who sentenced Him to the cross knew well His accusers 'had delivered him for envy'.

Nothing could prove more decisively or dramatically the personal forcefulness of Jesus, nor the immediate impression of prevailing power which He made on shrewd observers than the fact that a poor and humble Galilæan so quickly filled the great and learned of the land with envy and alarm, made even the mighty Caiaphas tremble on his ecclesiastical throne, and impelled the trembling hierarchy to combine in official and public action against Him, not only in violation of ordinary justice, but also in violation of the specific provisions of their own established law. But they who felt Jesus' power most strongly were those who knew Him best. His disciples opened their hearts to His influence, and knew by a continuous personal experience how penetrating and constructive this power was. They found, too, that this power did not depend upon His presence. The authority of an earthly conqueror, Napoleon or an Alexander, ceases with his life and the empire he has won is assailed and divided and soon passes utterly away. But Jesus foretold that His disciples would be able to do greater works after He was taken from them than they had done while He was with them. Till His death was accomplished He was—He said—straitened: His influence was confined. When He was dead and they were deprived of His presence, this influence seemed to be poured upon them in a greater flood of generosity, as though the clouds had passed away and the spiritual sunshine shed its rays upon them in the fullness of uninterrupted splendour.

However great the tributes in the Gospels to the power manifested by Jesus, those in the epistles and the apocalypse are greater still. Paul emphasised always that the Christian message was one of power and imparted power: one remembers 'the kingdom of God is not in word, but in power'. (I Cor. iv. 20.) 'God gave us not a spirit of fearfulness but of power.' The properties of Christ which are kept in prominence are prevailingly those of victory, might and dominion—of terror and of awfulness. He is the Lord of Glory, the Prince of the kings of the earth Who has made believers priests and kings unto God. He is the Saviour, the Redeemer, the Judge of all men, and in His hands are the keys of hell and death. He is the effulgence of the glory of God, the image of the Divine Essence, and upholds all things by the word of His power. He is the power of God and the wisdom of God, through Whom God made the world, and He now sitteth on the right hand of the Majesty on high in the heavenly places, far above all rule and authority and power and dominion and every name that is named, not only in this world but also in that which is to come. (Hebrews. 3; Eph. i. 19.)

This power of Christ has from the beginning been the constant Christian tradition and vital Christian belief through the ages. It was this power which within not many years of His death carried the tidings of His dominion farther to east and west than any Roman eagles ever penetrated. It was this power which has founded and developed a vast and mighty civilisation, which through many centuries inspired artists and statesmen, poets and legislators, which uplifted the ideals and improved the character of men and of nations, which lifted the names of His humblest disciples to a place of honour above the proudest kings. But for that benign and creative power the history of the West would have been incalculably different, and whatever is to be found in it of justice and kindness and goodwill would be wholly absent from its lampless and melancholy pages. Jesus was Himself, in His lifetime, the most lowly and simple of men, content with poverty, and not desirous of exerting personal lordship over His fellow-men. He ruled by service and self-sacrifice. Yet in all the glory and majesty accorded to Him in after ages, in all the extension and the magnificence of His dominion, there is nothing that goes beyond His own assertion of His true dignity, nothing that surpasses the homage and reverence which with His Own lips he urged to be His due. Identifying Himself with the cause of God on earth, He demanded of everyone immediate, exact and complete obedience. No other claim was to qualify or to come before this claim to man's service. When He said 'Follow me' the disciple arose, left all and followed Him. 'He that loveth father or mother more than me is not worthy of me; and he that loveth son or daughter more than me is not worthy of me. And he that doth not take his cross and follow after me, is not worthy of me.' (Matt. x. 37–38.) 'Whosoever he be of you that renounceth not all that he hath, he cannot be my disciple.' (Luke xiv. 33.) He was the Judge of all. It was His right to decide finally the moral worth of men's lives and to determine their destiny: there was no appeal, not even to God the Father. All things had been committed by the Father into the hands of the Son, and this trust had been given Him not as to a Saint, but as to one who was more than man. He was the sole revealer of God to man.

Only through Him could men see God or come to God. And yet, however much men loved Him and however ardently they strove to follow Him, they could not understand or appreciate or measure Him as they could one of their own fellow-men: He was different—not wholly beyond our reach, but assuredly beyond our grasp: 'No man knoweth the Son save the Father.' The utmost knowledge we may attain of Him is too little, is less than the truth, and however close to our hearts we may hold His perfections, His essential being is beyond our ken, and we belong to a lower order of existence than He.

These superhuman and divine claims were borne out in a way, subtle but unmistakable, by the manner of His approach to Truth. He said once that He was the Truth. His intellectual attitude was unique. No one in the Græco-Roman culture which under His influence was so soon to pass away, and no one in the civilisation which He was to found, ever assumed towards Truth the position assumed by Him, nor taught in the manner in which He taught. He did not present His philosophy of life in the same sort of way as did Socrates or Plato or Aristotle before Him, nor Seneca nor Kant nor any other after Him. He was noted from His childhood for His wisdom. As a boy He was strong in spirit, filled with wisdom, and as He grew in years He was described as increasing in wisdom. He said once (in effect) that His Gospel, and the preparation for it by the Baptist, were decreed and ordered by a transcendent wisdom which the faithful, though not perhaps the children of disobedience, would be able to appreciate and approve.

The body of His teaching, regarded in its completeness, is marked by a sublime intellectual coherence and forms a single self-consistent whole. His followers learned from Him to prove all things, hold fast that which is true. He Himself taught the multitudes to think, to use their reason, to watch the phenomena of Nature and consider how they would find in it rational ground for trust in God's care for humanity. He expressly directed His disciples, when He gave them the task of spiritualising the pagan souls of men, to be wise as serpents; and the gifts He promised with which they would overcome the superstition and secularism of the world were eloquence and wisdom. But He did not teach in the manner of one of the Wise Men of Judæa or of Greece. He did not present conclusions from experience or from observation or from learning. The first quality noticed about the authority with which He spoke was its originality. It was quite different from anything the people had ever heard, and they had heard much. Jesus did not begin with the known, the familiar, the accepted and draw inferences from it. He began with the unknown and on His own authority revealed it. He did not present a chain of argument. His aim was not merely to convince people's minds; it was that, but more also. It was to uplift character and produce action.

Though He taught men to seek the truth with open minds and fearless hearts, He did not Himself appear as a truth seeker. He did not speak as one who while He spoke was seeking the truth, nor even as one who having previously sought the truth had by enquiry found it, and was now able to present what he had found. He spoke, on the contrary, as a man who knew the truth by direct perception. The truth lay open before Him. He was one with it—was identified with it: as He said, He was the truth. He was able to give the instantaneous perfect answer to fit whatever occasion might present itself. He brought the white light of the whole truth to bear on any question. He was the intellectual light of the world which shines forth in its fullness on all objects. If one traced back to its source any shaft of daylight that falls on the earth, one would reach the sun; in the same way, any pronouncement of Jesus followed back to its origin would lead to the very heart of truth. Thus He speaks not merely with complete conviction but with mastery, with serene certainty. In this, no thinker or teacher in the whole range of His Dispensation approaches Him. His mental and moral attitude towards the doubts and difficulties that afflict us, is that of one outside them: He may share them with us through His sympathy, but He does not experience them. He dwells always in the light. He looks on our problems as one in heaven might look upon the earth. He is above them, external to them, His gaze surrounds them. He does not speak *ex cathedra* but *ex cælo.* We aspire towards heaven; we descry an ideal far above us in the skies. He brings the ideal down to us and imparts it as a command. His knowledge of truth is not such as reason ever could arrive at. He is not a teacher and educator merely in a human sense. He is also a revealer of something which reason never could discover and of the existence of which, perhaps, it might never think. Jesus taught some truths which had been deliberately hidden by God from man, and were now disclosed by degrees, as God pleased and by God's initiative. Man could never find them out by his own uninspired effort. The Gospel shows that further truths remain yet hidden from men, to be revealed in the future, and it hints at the nature of these truths. But these truths never can be known without divine initiative and divine grace.

Christ not only reveals new realms of experience and knowledge otherwise inaccessible, but He rouses to activity dormant powers in man, higher faculties as yet unused and undeveloped. He enlarges human consciousness. He shows creative power as the Word of God. He lifts to a new and loftier plane men's conceptions of life and duty. He opens new purposes in life, new fields of human endeavour. And by the exercise of such powers He proves Himself to be, as Christians have always held and as He Himself asserted, a Vicegerent of the Lord of Evolution, a Being altogether apart from anyone else in His Dispensation.

CHAPTER VII

THE SUCCESSION OF REVELATIONS

The majesty of Christ, His stupendous claims and the evidence of His power which the passing centuries brought, dazzled the imagination of the Christian public, and there arose by degrees a view of His place in the history of religion which may have suited well enough distant days of ignorance, but is not tenable in modern times. Thinking men know it to be mistaken, but they have not yet found an alternative which does not seem to detract from the dignity of Christ and to be inconsistent with His claims.

Speaking broadly, the Christian community has not believed and does not now believe in a continuous and world-embracing scheme of Revelation in which Jesus Christ played a part.

The existence of such a vast divine Design might in the past have been denied; and perhaps the idea of it would have been to many without value or meaning.

Nor has the Christian community believed that the Bible teaches a progressive system of Revelation which began with the creation of man and has been constantly guiding the race forward towards the attainment of a spiritual maturity. It has not believed in the gradual spiritual growth of the whole human race down through the ages, aided by a succession of heavenly Messengers.

No doubt with the thought of magnifying the position of Christ, and certainly with the effect of magnifying its own opinions, it has suffered Jesus of Nazareth to eclipse utterly all other Teachers; it has regarded His spiritual teaching as exhaustive and final, and has attributed to Him a personal immortality of some such corporeal kind as the pagans of old might have attributed to one of their gods like Apollo.

Such conceptions as these, though not indeed contained in the formal creeds of Christendom, have come down through tradition and are generally held, and either implied or expressed in much of the greatest Christian literature.

But their seeds were sown by men in less enlightened times than ours, and they flourished in the Dark Ages. They are not taught by Christ. They are now difficult to reconcile with known truth. They do not add to the magnificence of Christ's station, and they are seen to be derogatory to the character of Almighty God.

They are parallel to the views which the Hebrews in Jesus' time held about Moses. For the scribes taught that Moses' Revelation was complete and conclusive, that it would not receive nor need development and that a formal profession of Mosaism was enough to exalt a man above the rest of humanity. Because they accepted Moses in this sense, therefore they rejected Jesus. Mosaism, they thought, was enough, was final; why should they listen to a new teaching? This narrowness, this lack of openness of mind, we condemn in them as a heinous sin, and it led them to the appalling crime of martyring Jesus. And if the record of their error be written for our learning, it contains a warning against being in religion self-opinionated and unprogressive.

A narrow view of Revelation has for us greater difficulties than for them, and there is for us even less excuse for holding it. What knowledge had they compared with ourselves of the vast extent of the globe with all its seas and lands, of the number and variety of the peoples that inhabit it, of the civilisations and religions that had sprung up and flourished and perhaps already decayed in that great continent of Asia in which they dwelt; what did they know of the antiquity of the earth and of humanity, what conception had they of such truths as progress and evolution?

A wider knowledge has brought us a severer responsibility.

We who compose universal histories, who study comparative religion, who can take a far broader and more discerning view of the ancient world than was possible for those who themselves lived in it, we, thus highly privileged, have no excuse at all for prejudice or egoism in our interpretation of Christ and His mission.

The dogma, the notion that there is no single divine law governing continuously the affairs of men whether before or after Christ, that in some inexplicable way and for no imaginable reason the compassion and the redemptive love of the Heavenly Father was shut away through millenniums from all His children, that the multitudes were left during those ages in some outer cold and darkness, were expected to shift for themselves without divine guidance, to submit themselves blindly to the chances and changes of an orphaned and undirected world, and that nations and individuals moved on their aimless way without instruction of conscience, without the inspiration and the cheer which religion confers, without access to knowledge of spiritual truth—any such dogma or notion as this seems to us strange and arbitrary to a degree, an evident invention of man's cruel and uninstructed imagination. There is not a word of evidence for it in the teachings of Christ. It is wholly repugnant to that teaching. It is the merest superstition. Indeed, it is worse than untenable and monstrous; it is assuredly blasphemous, an insult to the character and power of God. What but the evil thought of man could imagine that a God of justice and compassion, of succour and helpfulness, the Author of all that is kind and good, would create the human race and abandon them to dwell unshepherded without the comfort of His Word or the light and warmth of His presence through innumerable ages till at last that year dawned which we in the West denominate the year One. Has God ever shut the gates of mercy against His children?

If it be argued that He has and that He showed His clemency and forgiveness by opening these gates in the year One, the special question arises—why, that year in particular? What distinction is there about that epoch to make it suitable to the exclusion of all other epochs for the one and only effort of God to illuminate and save mankind? Great saints arose and mighty civilisations flourished before that period, and left an enduring mark on the memory and conscience of mankind. And since that time Islám produced its wonderful mystics and that brilliant civilisation to which we of to-day owe so large a debt.

What intelligible or consistent philosophy of world-history can be woven around the idea that the one authentic Revelation of God was given nineteen hundred years ago, and that it was both final and complete? None at all. This idea originated in days of ignorance, and bears every mark of the date of its origin. It contradicts the teaching of Christ and the spirit of the Bible; it is incompatible with the revealed character of God and repugnant to the better instincts and to the fuller knowledge of our time.

If the interpretation of the Bible as the story of mankind's spiritual evolution did not bring into relief the reality of Redemption, did not enhance the majesty of Christ and uplift our conception of the glory of the Creator, still one would be impelled to accept it since it is proved from the Bible's own words. But why should anyone be reluctant or hesitate to accept it since it redounds to the greater glory of God and His Messengers and all His works! How precious in such a world of doubt as ours is the picture of a scheme of salvation which is intelligible and in accord with the rest of our thinking and which shows how real and grave and costly and perilous are those imperfections and sins which men in ignorance so long have treated as of no account!

How great, how far beyond the thought of any generation of men is this Scheme which Christ unfolds!

How wonderful the love and wisdom that could conceive and order it!

How unimaginable the Power that commands and creates, that informs every part of this vast process from everlasting to everlasting and that executes His plan throughout according to a purpose defined before the first foundation of the world! How far surpassing anything we can ever know of glory is One who is styled the Son of so great a God, the Image of His perfections, the executive of His authority over all things in heaven and earth!

Jesus was not called on to draw any full sketch of the Redemptive Scheme of God nor to delineate it in any detail, as is done, for instance, in the *Book of Certitude*. The view of it which He offers to us may be compared to our view of the young crescent moon. A portion of the moon's orb corresponding to the Christian gospel, is seen in full light; the rest is shown in outline by a faint filament of thin light so that the eye can trace the size and contour of the moon, but nothing more.

Christ was talking to a child-people, and He had no opportunity of expanding a philosophy of the General Design of God. Doubtless this was one of those larger mysteries for the revelation of which their minds were not yet ripe. 'Other things I have to tell you, but ye cannot bear them now.'

Nevertheless the discourses of Christ are shot through with allusions and references to the course of God's evolutionary plan. Many of His words take on a richer, deeper meaning when contemplated against the background of the General Design. Only when His teaching is examined as part of a progressive revelation, when it is seen to be calculated to answer a particular need of mankind at a given time and to carry humanity over a definite stage of their evolutionary journey—only then can the teaching be recognised as having its own shape and pattern, as being a consistent and ordered whole, a considered prescription fitted to the spiritual malady of a special age.

Not until the Gospel is so regarded can the wisdom of Christ or His power be really appreciated. Jesus made several references to other revelations, past or future, than His own. But there is one in particular which is of special significance because in it when His authority is challenged by certain Jews He asserts the spiritual continuity of His own revelation with the earlier revelations of pre-Hebrew days. 'Jesus said unto them, Verily, verily, I say unto you, Before Abraham was, I am.' (John viii. 58.) The Jews took this to refer to Jesus the son of Mary who stood before them; they thought accordingly He was mocking them. Believers know that He spoke not of the individual Jesus but of the Eternal Christ. The Christ, the Word of God which spoke through Jesus, which was as a Sun, the splendours of which were reflected in Jesus as in a mirror, had spoken to men long before the prophet Abraham; it had not confined its energies, its appearances, its utterances to the Hebrews alone. The Revelation of God through the eternal Word antedated the Jewish race and had been in action untold ages ago. Jesus gave no backward limit of time. He said that Revelation had been in process before Jewish history began and had always been one and the same, always in source and spirit identical with that which now was vouchsafed through Jesus of Nazareth.

Jesus was not called on to particularise further than this. He utterly denied the arrogant monopoly claimed by the self-righteous Hebrews and—as his way was—in so doing, revealed to men a truth with a far profounder significance than appeared on the surface.

While Jesus here and elsewhere stressed the unity and wholeness of all Revelation He emphasised in particular and with detail one portion of God's revelatory design—namely, His own succession to Moses, the nature of the transition from one Dispensation to the other, and the relationship established between the two connected but different Teachings.

This was to the Hebrew a matter of vital importance. It has to us to-day as students of the unified Design of God a further interest. From it, if we study it with humility and attention, we may be able to discover the principle of succession which imparts continuity to a Movement that is carried forward by a series of separate impulses. We may, for instance, be able to form some idea of the kind of spiritual relationship which must have existed between the work of Abraham and that of Moses who followed him, and perhaps be able to estimate what kind of change and advance beyond the First Teaching of Christ will be brought to mankind in His Second Advent.

CHAPTER VIII

THE RELATION OF CHRIST TO MOSES

'We have Moses and the prophets. Are not they good enough for us? What need have we of this new teaching? Why should we listen to this new prophet?' Such would be the remark of every Jewish churchman as he heard the counsels and pronouncements of Jesus of Galilee. Jesus anticipated the objection. From the first He tried to make clear to all Hebrew enquirers what was the relation of His own message to that of His great predecessor. But His teaching on this point has more than a temporal or local meaning and is of interest and value to-day to the modern Christian and to every student of progressive revelation.

The people to whom Jesus delivered His message were Hebrews. They were steeped in Mosaism: how strong its grip upon them their subsequent history shows. Their whole outlook on life, their whole civilisation, was penetrated by Mosaism. Passionately religious, intensely nationalistic, they regarded themselves as apart from the rest of mankind, and the force which united them in this exclusiveness was their loyalty to Moses. A man of any other nationality, a Greek or a Roman, might in those days travel to foreign lands and bring his gods with him or find abroad a faith kindred to his own. But to the Jews of the Dispersion as to those (fewer in number) who remained at home, there was only one true God, the God Who spoke to them through Moses; only one priesthood, that which had come from Moses; only one Temple, that in Jerusalem, in which sacrifices for the forgiveness of sins and for fellowship with God were continually offered according to the ritual of Moses. Jews out of every nation under heaven mingling with their brethren of Galilee and Judæa thronged the courts of that Temple, the shrine and sacred centre of their history and their religion, where they gathered under the shadow of that divine prophet who had delivered them from Egyptian serfdom, led them to the Holy Land and made of them a nation chosen by the one true God as His very own.

From Moses, too, and after him from the prophets of his Dispensation, flowed that distinctive glorious hope that animated all Hebrew hearts, fortifying and cheering them in adversity and proving itself too strong to be quenched by any vicissitude or lapse of time: the hope of the Messiah.

Every detail of Hebrew life, public or private or domestic, was regulated with precise and prying exactitude by the enactments of the Law which (some of it oral and some of it written) was all supposed to have been given on Mount Sinai by God to Moses. The 'traditions of the elders' explained, expanded and applied to every imaginable case the meaning of Scripture; so great was the veneration in which they were held that they were regarded as more binding than the written Word, and once they were formed and accepted as orthodox not a phrase or letter might be annulled or changed. The most important and prominent persons in the social order were not officers of the army nor leading politicians, but rather the Pharisees, a religious party who kept ostentatiously the minutiæ of the law of Moses, and the Scribes who were the official expounders of that law. A scribe's dignity was so exalted that he outweighed in value all the common people and any statement whatever that he made was above question and must be received with implicit belief.

The Mosaic religion, as it confronted Jesus, was thus a great system pervading all Hebrew activities; it was final, closed and unassailable. In the midst of it stood the written Law; around it the sacrosanct traditions; and on the outside guarding this holy deposit walked the sentinel-figures of the Scribes whose authority none could challenge and who were the intimates of God both in this world and in the next.

When Jesus came to bestow a new revelation on the Hebrews, He did not find an open door into their hearts, nor their minds hungry for further knowledge and for a better righteousness. Quite the contrary. As a teacher who was courteous to those He addressed, who respected the opinions of others and who desired not to over-awe nor overwhelm nor to coerce, but to attract and to win, to persuade and to convince, His first pedagogical problem was to find the best approach to souls already saturated with an alien orthodoxy. He showed no wish to remove the law and the teaching of Moses from their minds: heaven forbid. His aim was to cleanse away the accretions which had accumulated about it; to straighten out what through men's perversity had been warped; to make people's belief in Moses sincere and true—not a view adopted by inheritance, but a view firmly held by a native activity of the believer's own heart. He took for granted the divine prophethood of Moses; upheld the truth of Moses' revelation, and represented His own teaching as a natural development out of it.

But His words on this matter have a wider reference

than their immediate appeal and a larger purpose than to remove the religious difficulties of those to whom He spoke. They prove to be an important part of His gospel and to illumine the method which God has established on earth for the spiritual evolution of mankind. They testify to the continuity of revealed religion and show how one revelation passes away and enters into that which succeeds it. He said (in effect) that between His Message and that of Moses there was an organic connexion. Though He might alter the customs of Moses, yet He was not Moses' enemy but his friend; He was not poisoning, not subverting the ancient Word but purifying it, advancing it: if the Scribes really knew as much about Moses as they imagined they knew, they would understand that Moses and He both bare witness to the same Truth, upheld the same cause and had in view the same consummation of human history.

His attitude on this point was wholly new and surprising. It not only affronted the prejudices of the Scribes, the Pharisees and the ultra conservative, but it perplexed the disciples themselves and remained for long a critical difficulty to Christian converts from Judaism.

John the Baptist had already prepared the mind of the Jewish people for the new point of view. He connected his work closely with the Old Testament, claimed to fulfil the prophecy of Isaiah and to be 'the voice of one crying in the wilderness'. In spirit and in manner he was like Elijah of old, with whom Jesus identified him. But in trenchant, fiery phrases he rejected utterly the current interpretations of God's Word and the authority of its self-appointed expounders. The Pharisees and Sadducees considered themselves the elect of the elect, the choicest spirits of the chosen people; but when they came to him to seek his baptism, they did not receive from him any congratulations either on the reality of their holiness or the reality of their repentance. He greeted them as a 'generation of vipers', as deadly ingrates who being cradled in Mosaism, drawing out of it for themselves honours and privileges, were yet the treacherous enemies of the system that supported them, living at the heart of it and striking at its heart. He denounced their pride of race, their trust in their descent from Abraham. He bade them if they repented to show their repentance by their deeds; for there was about to descend upon them from on high a greater baptism than his, the baptism of One Who with unerring judgment would separate the true Hebrew from the false, the true shepherd from the hireling; and if their repentance and their deeds were not approved by this Holy One, He would assuredly expose them and cast them out to a terrible destruction.

So far the Baptist went in his teaching; and it was far. He repudiated without qualification or compromise as utterly worthless all the Masters of Israel and everything they did: they were the covert, sneaking, treacherous enemies of the Great Deliverer on whose revelation they fattened themselves and nothing less than a renunciation of all their past pride and wickedness could save them from judgment. As the forerunner of the Christ, preparing for his Lord a way into men's hearts, he had to break the people's mental idols, to clear away ecclesiastic debris, and to present first the negative destructive side of the new teaching. Jesus followed, taking exactly the same attitude towards Moses and the Old Testament as John, but presenting the positive aspect of John's argument and laying as it were the foundations of His system on the ground which John had cleared.

The effect of the Gospel of Jesus has been in history to spread the knowledge of the Old Testament far and wide across the globe, to win for it a place of reverence and love in countless millions of human hearts and to make the name of Moses honoured among all the peoples, nations and languages of the earth. The enthusiasm of the Scribes and Pharisees did not accomplish this: far otherwise. It has been the direct result of the teaching of Jesus Who Himself bound up His own work with that of Moses and bade all Christians down the ages to esteem and glorify Moses as His own predecessor and one of the exalted eternal prophets of the Most High God. So transcendent was the veneration which the first Christians learned from their Lord to pay to Moses that not only do New Testament writers so strongly stress the debt of Christianity to him, but in the apocalyptic vision of the final Day of Wrath of God those who have gotten the victory over the powers of evil sing to the music of the harps of God a lyric of triumph in which the Song of Moses still blends at that distant day with the Song of the Lamb.

> And they sing the song of Moses the servant of God, and the song of the Lamb, saying, Great and marvellous *are* thy works, Lord God Almighty; just and true *are* thy ways, thou King of saints. (Rev. xv. 3.)

Strange that both the orthodox Hebrews on the one side, and Christ upon the other should so honour Moses and yet their views should be irreconcileable and violently opposed to each other. What the Jewish authorities thought of Jesus' attitude to Moses is made plain by their actions. Jesus on His side denied that the Jews for all their parade of devotion really believed in Moses at all; He said the hope they placed in Moses was vain—He was not on their side, He was against them; true faith was impossible for them because they sought only glory from one another, not from God. If He said these hard things of them, it was in fact not Himself but Moses who was their accuser. (John v. 42–47.)

On the other hand, Jesus claimed that between Him and Moses, in their teaching, their function, their purpose, there was the closest resemblance and affinity. The vision vouchsafed to the three principal disciples on the Mount of Transfiguration revealed in symbol the intimate spiritual communion which Christ enjoyed with Moses in moments of contemplation.

On one occasion (John xiv. 7) Jesus said that to know Him was to know the Father, and again, whosoever had seen Him had seen the Father: He was the express image of God reflecting in perfection all the divine attributes. On another occasion, speaking to the Jews, He said that if one believed in Moses one would believe in Him, the Christ; meaning that so alike were He and Moses in those things which the eye of Faith discerns that a true believer would see no difference between them. In these two comparisons, first of His likeness to God and second of Moses' likeness to Him, Jesus shows that the essential kinship between Himself and Moses was in their godlike attributes, in their perfections, in their power, in their service of God and in the spirit of their teaching. They were two distinct individuals, separated by more than a thousand years, and they gave counsels and commandments which in many ways were different; yet in their spirit and their power they were so much alike that sincere true-hearted belief in one was identical with belief in the other.

In such passages as these Jesus makes manifest how spiritual evolution is for ever continuous through unceasing change, and how one Prophet of God succeeding another shows forth by word and by example a Truth which in its aspect and in the degree of its revelation is always altering, but in its source and in its essence is for ever the same. The progress of religion appears in the Bible as being analogous to the growth of an individual, to the process of a child's becoming a man. From infancy to old age the human body is being unceasingly transformed, its appearance is changing, and its development in youth is so rapid that the passage of ten years or less will alter a child beyond recognition. Intellectual capacity, too, develops with the years, the individual's knowledge increases, his character is ennobled: and yet his identity remains the same throughout. So is it with the religion of mankind which the Bible portrays. Religion becomes progressively a larger and sublimer thing; but it remains in essence one and the same religion. The sacred rites and ceremonies, the customs and ordinances of one era are cast aside in another, and new rites and customs substituted for them, but the same religion remains, expressing itself more fully in new forms. The Divine Prophets follow one another, each with an ampler Revelation than his predecessor, but all coming from the One God, exemplifying in word and deed the one Truth and acting as the Lord's vicegerents in one evolutionary process, one Scheme of Salvation.

Each prophet is independent of any before him, annuls or institutes ordinances and rites as he sees fit, expands or adds to doctrine, and under God issues new decrees on his own authority and in his own name. But his informing purpose is none other than to carry on the divine work of his predecessor: to fulfil, not to destroy.

The Gospel gives with emphasis many illustrations in detail of this great and vital truth, and enforces it strongly by holding always over against it the utterly false and mischievous idea on the continuity of religion held by the Pharisees and the Scribes.

There are certain fundamental spiritual truths which stand in both Revelations; some of which may have come down without any change from earlier prophets than Moses. Such truths are, for example, first, that of the existence and the unity of God; second, that of God's two prerogatives, to command and to create (all men being no more than his servants and his creatures); third, that of the two laws of love and of justice; fourth, that of revelation and prophethood (for Moses foretold there would come after him another Moses, from which statement arose the Messianic expectation fulfilled in the Advent of Christ). The truth of personal immortality might be added to the list of essential truths, for Jesus affirmed that Moses had by implication taught it, though a lack of spiritual acumen had prevented the Hebrews from discerning the significance of his words.

Such everlasting verities as these form as it were the core of revealed religion as it appears in the two testaments. On the other hand the Gospel shows almost from the first word to the last in how many ways the teaching of Jesus was more lofty, more exacting and more subtle than that which Moses had given in an earlier day to a cruder people.

Moses addressed himself to the Twelve Tribes and said, 'Hear, O Israel, the statutes and judgments which I speak in your ears . . .' (Deut. v. i, etc.) Jesus bade His disciples teach all nations, spoke of His gospel being preached throughout the world and foretold men would come into the Kingdom from north and south, from east and west.

Moses summarised his teaching in Ten Commandments; and when the Christian peruses them he observes that Christ heightened each several one of these and did not leave one of them unamended. Moses had said the Israelites were to have one God only. Jesus went further: He said that all mankind was to have one God, the Universal Father of all men and nations. Moses forbade the people to grave any image lest they fall down and worship it; but Jesus said a man must have nothing in his heart to worship but God only. Moses warned men against taking God's name in vain, an injunction which has a general meaning and also a special reference to keeping a solemn oath. Jesus went further: He put the command in a positive form—men were to hold God's name and His attributes holy. He forbade an oath as wrong in principle because it implied that reliance should not be put on a man's bare word and in effect condoned a simple untruth. Moses separated the Sabbath, the seventh day, from the rest of the week as a day to be kept holy. Jesus taught that all time was God's; and as the early Christians had not, like the Hebrews, a central Temple, but found God present everywhere if they worshipped in sincerity and truth, so they set no special days apart as holier than others. Moses said, 'Honour thy father and thy mother', and to obedience to this injunction he attached a promise —'that thy days may be long upon the land . . .' Jesus said that a higher duty even than that to earthly parents is owed to one's Father in heaven, that one may have to leave father and mother for God's sake, and He averred that a man has in reality no true Father except the Father in heaven who is his Creator. 'And call no *man* your father upon the earth: for one is your Father, which is in heaven.' (Matt. xxiii. 9.) The first recorded act of Jesus was to leave Joseph and Mary that He might go to the Temple and 'be about his Father's business'. Moses forbade the taking of another man's life or his property or his wife; Jesus would not permit any thought or emotion or desire in the heart that would lead to any such wrong deed. Moses prohibited the coveting of anything of one's neighbours. Jesus extended indefinitely the meaning of 'neighbour', and He did not stop short at forbidding any coveting of another man's goods, but he strongly enjoined a readiness to part with one's own goods for the benefit of those in need, regardless of race or creed.

As in these precepts and counsels, so through all the teaching of the New Testament may be traced the two-fold principle of spiritual continuity and change on which progress in religion depends and through which the evolution of the spirit of man is achieved. Jesus with definiteness and with firmness rescinded or altered very much that Moses had enjoined. He heightened the former level of moral obligation. He extended the range of spiritual knowledge. He abolished Old Testament ceremonies and forms, laws and customs, and introduced others (simpler and fewer in number) in their stead.

The importance attached by Jesus to these changes is shown by the fact that for them He faced the hatred and the opposition of the all-powerful Scribes and Pharisees and made inevitable that martyrdom which brought His work to so cruel and untimely an end before the disciples had received that instruction and training of which they stood in such great need.

But if the life of Jesus and the record of it be brief, there is material enough for the believer to study the relation between the Teaching of Jesus and the Teaching of Moses, to ponder over the changes which Jesus made and from them to learn what is essential in religion and what not, and so to judge in what respects future religious progress is to be made. However little human judgment can decide this question, one principle is established for ever and one mistake exposed beyond cavil by the error of the Scribes and Pharisees. They entertained no doubt whatever that the continuity of revealed religion depended on the rites, ceremonies, customs and ordinances given by the Prophet, and through these its reality was conveyed for ever. Through this delusion they were prevented from recognising the need of a New Teaching, and when One came in the very spirit and power of Moses (and even greater power) they tried Him by their own standards and adjudged their own Messiah an imposter, a friend of the devil's.

CHAPTER IX

THE INDEPENDENCE OF CHRIST

The Grand Redemptive Scheme of God carried forward through the process of spiritual evolution is shown in the Bible as a perfectly co-ordinated whole. Every part of it has its special place, its special use. And each one of these parts not only contributes to the completeness of the general scheme, but is itself a unit and within its own limits is in itself complete.

If Jesus asserted the continuity of His teaching with that of Moses, in words at least as emphatic He affirmed its independence and self-sufficiency. His mission was not that of a reformer. He was not an Isaiah nor a greater Malachi. The Old Testament had already made it clear that there are two separate ranks of prophets, a lower and a higher. Of the lower it is said that to him God shows himself in a vision or speaks in a dream; with the higher God holds direct communion and speaks immediately. Moses belonged to the latter of higher order, and therefore stood apart from all the other lesser prophets and seers of his time and Dispensation. When Moses predicted that God would raise up 'a Prophet . . . like unto me' he did not refer to a prophet of the second rank, to an Isaiah or a Jeremiah, but to a supreme prophet of his own degree, the lord of a Dispensation. (Num. xii. 6 ff.; Deut. xviii. 15.)

The significance of Moses' words and the essential difference between the two ranks of prophethood is brought out even more fully in the New Testament than in the Old.

The station of the Hebrew prophets is indeed exalted and sublime; but the superiority of the Prophet of Nazareth to even the greatest of the prophets of Israel is manifold and immeasurable. They were, it is true, like unto Him in some respects: they were not ordained as inheritors of a formal succession; they did not receive their authority from men; they were personally commissioned by God Himself in some mystical manner. But the prophet of Israel would declare, 'Hear ye the word of the Lord', or 'Thus saith the Lord': while Jesus would say, 'It hath been said by them of old time, but I say unto you'; or 'A new commandment I give to you'. The ancient prophet gave in God's name counsels or commands in some special crisis or emergency; but he did not give a complete revelation of ordered truth, nor did he give a world-wide message; he did not abrogate any of the Mosaic statutes or ordinances; he did not found a new religious system, institute new rites and civil laws, ordain disciples to take the place of the former priesthood and entrust to them supreme spiritual authority on earth. The ancient prophet foretold the coming of a king, a deliverer, a Messiah; but he did not claim that he was himself the fulfilment of earlier prophecies nor declare in public or in private that he was the Messiah. Nor would any ancient prophet presume to make such statements as these of Jesus, that His Father had delivered all things unto Him (Matt. xi. 27), and hath given Him authority over all flesh (John xvii. 2) even to the extent of executing judgment upon them (John v. 27).

How glorious and sublime the real status of the Lord

Christ was, we mortals never shall be able to understand or to divine, for these ætherial mysteries lie above the range of human comprehension. But we can with the utmost certainty perceive that He dwelt in a height of power exalted far above that of an Isaiah or of a Daniel. The angels at His birth announced Him as a Saviour; while He was yet an infant the aged Simeon recognised in His birth the coming of God's salvation to mankind; and His invitation 'Come unto me' was an offer of redemption to all the world. No longer in the name of Moses, but now in the Name of Christ, the Jews—and all mankind likewise—were henceforth to seek deliverance from sin and access to God's pleasure. In Jesus' Name men were to be saved, and whatever was now necessary for salvation was to be found in His teaching.

Jesus made it clear that His mission was not only independent and self-sufficient, but that it had also its definite function; it served a special and bounded purpose. It had its assigned beginning and its assigned conclusion. As at the nearer end it fitted the Mosaic Revelation, so at the further end it was to fit the future Revelation of the Second Advent.

The mission with which Moses was entrusted is exhibited in the Old Testament with some clearness. His task was to deliver the Israelites from their bitter bondage in Egypt and lead them to the Land of Canaan, a land flowing with milk and honey, which had been promised to their forefathers Abraham, Isaac and Jacob. This he was to do through the express might of God, Who would reveal Himself to Moses under a New Name—meaning that Moses would give to the people a fuller revelation of God's nature than had been given them before.

In order to accomplish this work Moses was obliged to take command of the whole Israelitish people and to assume the entire burden of leadership both in war and in peace. He was organiser, administrator, executive, law-giver, spokesman as well as general-in-chief against all hostile tribes.

Jesus' personal task had no such material aim as that of Moses. He was not to lead the people to an actual Land of Promise, but to a heavenly city, to the Kingdom of God. The lofty and intense spirituality which distinguished His mission is shown by the whole tenor of His teaching and especially by such pronouncements as 'Behold the Lamb of God, which taketh away the sin of the world' (John i. 29); 'I am the resurrection, and the life' (John xi. 25); 'I am the bread of life' (John vi. 35); 'I am the way, the truth, and the life . . .' (John xiv. 6.)

'To this end was I born and to this end am I come into the world, to bear witness to the truth.'

Jesus testified that the work on earth entrusted to Him was not indefinite nor discursive, but was to a degree marked out beforehand by His Father. He spoke of the works that He did as being 'the works which the Father hath given me to accomplish' (John v. 36), and He stated that He sought not His own will, but the will of Him that sent Him (v. 30). In the Gospel of St. Matthew He defines the terms of His mission more precisely. Making as if to decline the request of a Canaanitish woman, He gives as a reason, 'I am not sent but unto the lost sheep of the house of Israel', where the word Israel must have its literal sense. When after calling the twelve He sent them out on their first mission He gave them the same restricted field of teaching.

> Go not into any way of the Gentiles, and enter not into any city of the Samaritans . . . But go rather to the lost sheep of the house of Israel. (Matt. x. 5-6; *see also* xv. 24.)

His Gospel was one of God's love for all mankind regardless of any bounds of country or race: 'God so loved the world . . .' He bade His disciples after His death, 'Go teach all nations'; and He foretold that His message would be carried to the ends of the earth. But He Himself, except for His sojourn as a small child in Egypt, never dwelt for any length of time outside of Palestine. He hardly crossed the boundaries of His own land and His great teaching tours were in Galilee and Judæa. He made no effort to do what He bade His disciples do, and what after His ascension they in fact did. He did not, as St. Paul did, journey forth to spread the Gospel far and wide throughout the Roman Empire. He was born, He lived and worked and died among the Jews. He chose as His apostles Jews only, and He evangelised the world through Jews.

The story of the Temptation (Matt. iv, Luke iv) shows strongly and vividly that in planning out the course of His life-work Jesus from the beginning had this restricted field of operation in plain view.

Jesus Himself told the story of His experience, and according to His usual practice He made mental images and abstract things more clear by shaping them into concrete form and presenting them as a parable. The event occurred on the vigil of His ministry. He had withdrawn alone into the wilderness and in concentrated thought was considering what means or policy He should adopt in order best to carry out among them the tremendous responsibility laid on Him by His Father.

The actual narrative of Jesus' life and work as given in the Bible makes known the course which Jesus chose and what came of that choice. The story of the Temptation shows that before He began His ministry other courses presented themselves to Jesus' mind; that He might have chosen one or more of these and that in that case the development of the Gospel on earth would have been along another line.

There alone in the wilderness He considered what various ways there were of approaching His great world-task, and which among these ways would be most pleasing to God.

He rejected at once any suggestion of letting any personal needs or desires influence His course; He set His face deliberately from the first towards the way of hunger and hardship and even—if need should be—of martyrdom.

As He contemplated the scope of the work which the Heavenly Father had entrusted to His care (extending as it did over the whole wide world in which whosoever believed on Him should be saved) His thoughts and His love stretched over all mankind and He wondered how He would win these uncountable multitudes to God. At once He rejected any suggestion of using means, however promising or tempting, that might not agree with the definitely spiritual mission He had received from His Father—means that in other circumstances would be in themselves permissible and right. Moses' task, though essentially religious, had been in large part material: his duty was to free his people from subjection to a foreign yoke and lead them out to a land which they should make their own. He found it obligatory to make himself a national deliverer and to organise and to rule with the strong hand of a military commander. But Jesus' task included no such practical commission; the administrative element was small and altogether secondary; He was 'to take away the sins of the world', to lead men towards the Kingdom of God, to open the gates of eternal life and bring into being on earth a new kind of spiritual fellowship transcending all material limits. The assumption of some kind of national leadership might have been permissible and necessary had some less spiritual world-objective been in view; but it was not for Him to seek material power. For Him, charged with a spiritual aim, to seek such power would have been unfitting, and He discarded it at once utterly as displeasing to God. He decided to use a purely spiritual appeal, to be a Divine Teacher, and to draw all men to Him by the force of His spiritual love.

It was in the Sacred Temple, in Jerusalem, in the centre of Hebrew religion and civilisation, that Jesus was to make His appearance and His appeal. How was He to attract the attention of these devoted and even fanatical religionaries, and to show forth His heavenly power with such effect that they would abandon the time-honoured Mosaic rites and statutes and accept from Him a new system of order and worship? Here again He rejected at once any suggestion that He should make an unspiritual approach to the hearts of the faithful or to their religious sense. He would not take any personal advantage of His extraordinary endowments. He would not disarm disbelief by any miraculous amazing display of His superiority, nor reduce all alike to a common submissiveness by cowing their imaginations.

No. Not by spectacle, nor by force, nor by any means save those of an utterly humble, selfless love, and spiritual power would He give His Message to the Hebrews and through them to all the kingdoms of the earth. Anything other than this would in His case be of the Evil One.

When the forty days were over and He returned from His solitary vigil in the wilderness, His course was laid out and He travelled straight forward in it till He was able to say upon the Cross, 'It is finished'.

Thus Scripture testifies that Jesus' mission on earth was in a general sense defined for Him by the Father; it reveals something of what the terms of that mission were; and it shows how Jesus before entering on His ministry thought out with care the principle of action He would follow in His enterprise.

Jesus' teachings are imbued with the same singleness of purpose and unity of spirit as all the rest of His life and work. They fall within a prearranged scheme. They are designed for a definite effect; they form a distinct pattern and convey a single spiritual impression. His manner in teaching was so simple and so spontaneous that it is easy not to discover how many depths of wisdom are hidden in His utterances. He Himself drew attention to this fact when He addressed Himself not to all who stood by, but only to those who had ears to hear, that is, had ears to receive His spiritual meaning. If, He said, there was one kind of heart which would truly mark, learn and inwardly digest His words, there were three several kinds (the hard heart, the shallow heart, the preoccupied heart) which could not. Only deep reverence and long familiarity can help the soul to realise that Jesus' simplicity was due to His entire mastery of His subject and to His being able to express the essence of truth in the most clear and appealing way.

So unstudied and artless are Jesus' utterances, often called forth by some sudden emergency or some casual question, that one may easily miss the fact that they all fall within a certain scheme, they are in their range and level chosen according to plan, and they form when taken together a unified whole. The presence not only of enthusiasm and kindness, but of restraint and of order and of method in His work, and the firm coherence of it all, becomes most clearly apparent when His teaching is not examined in isolation, but in relation to the rest of Scripture and in particular to the preceding Revelation of Moses. To regard His teaching in its true perspective as given in the Bible; to observe how it looks back to the teaching of the past and forward to the teaching of the future, is to be aided in seeing that whatever Jesus said was in strict accord with the commission He had received from God and with the plan which He had decided on for Himself. His own judgment fixed for Him how much He might bring forth out of the infinite treasury of God's truth and give to the people of His Dispensation. He gave to men knowledge which Moses had withheld; and He withheld knowledge at His First Advent which He might be able to give at His Second Advent. A strong will and a firm intellectual grasp determined the limits of His teaching. An utterly selfless spirit impelled Him to declare as much of the Truth as befitted the evolving capacity of the age without the least regard for the consequences to Himself.

To keep the Gospel of Jesus, when studied, in its determined place in the Bible, which means to keep it in its place in the spiritual evolution of mankind, is to be in the best position to interpret its many significances, both great and small.

There is yet one further relation in which the Gospel may be regarded, in addition to its relation to Mosaism and to the Second Advent and to the whole evolutionary scheme. It is a relation of lesser importance (it seems) than these; yet since it is indicated in Scripture and by the words of Christ Himself, it is not to be passed by: the relation of Jesus' teaching to that of Abraham and Moses taken together, as if His revelation in a particular sense summed up and consummated theirs. Abraham had founded a spiritual family. Moses founded a spiritual nation. Jesus spiritualised humanity.

Scripture suggests in several ways that the Master-Prophets Abraham, Moses and Christ are not only connected by a special tie of race and of place, but that also in some spiritual manner they form a distinct group, a threefold unity, and that their combined work constitutes a particular and crucial episode in the grand progress of human evolution. Their figures stand out far above all others in the Old and New Testaments: Abraham and Moses are the mightiest of the mighty, the sublimest heroes of the Old Testament; Christ is the divine hero of the New. While the sacred narrative covers the whole period of manhood's existence from the date of its birth to that of its spiritual maturity, the life and work of these three fill almost the whole book. In the twelfth chapter of Genesis there is a suggestion that God's call of Abraham marked a critical epoch, a new departure in the spiritual history of humanity. As the story proceeds everything is done that art can do to create a sense of suspense and expectancy, to arouse wonder and hope and forward-looking thoughts. In the Gospels the strongest claim is advanced that what men were taught to hope for had come, that what they had awaited was here. A hundred prophecies are quoted as fulfilled in Jesus, and Jesus endorses such quotations. Spiritually sensitive minds recognise intuitively in Jesus the Consolation of Israel. The heightening of the moral level of the Teaching is so marked that this climax is felt as reaching to the spiritual realm and as being an eternal fact. The awfulness of the mistake of those whose minds are dead to any sense of uplift and progress and who destroy as a malefactor the world's guide, enforces still further the reality of the climax.

Jesus emphasised on many occasions the continuity of His work with that of Moses; but on one occasion, in language so strange and challenging as to call for pause and special thought, He referred to the connexion between His own Dispensation and that of an earlier Prophet, of the predecessor of Moses, of the Father of the faithful, Abraham.

His statement, 'Your father Abraham rejoiced to see my day: and he saw *it*, and was glad' (John viii. 56), conveyed to His hearers at the time no intelligible meaning; one might wonder why He uttered it. The only effect was to mystify and exasperate. But to the faithful heart its significance is radiant and sublime. It shows that the great service which the Hebrew people through their saints and seers rendered to mankind and which is treated at large in the Bible, is to be regarded as a smaller system of Revelation within the larger system, as being in its lesser way a spiritual whole with three Master-Figures and three Parts, leading up to its climax and its highest glory in Christ. A fitting subject for so great a book as the Bible! Abraham, that majestic and lonely being of the ancient past, the Father of the Faithful, inaugurates under God's command a great religious movement. By that divine light which was his he saw in vision on the eternal plane (as lesser prophets in a later day saw less clearly than he) the Dawning and the Glory of the Day of Christ, the fulfilling in Christ's world-wide spiritual revelation of the work which he himself as a pioneer of God began two thousand years and more before. As on the material plane Moses had looked out from the mountain-top of Pisgah upon the Promised Land into which another than he would lead his people, so on the spiritual plane in a manner somewhat similar Abraham was privileged to see far off the Spiritual Land into which a sacred Son of the Hebrews was to lead mankind.

CHAPTER X

THE SPIRITUALISING OF MANKIND

In the Lord's Supper Christ gave a remembrance of Himself. In the Lord's Prayer He gave a remembrance of His work and teaching. The prayer was, of course, to be used; and not only to be used but to be copied. It was revealed expressly as a pattern prayer. It shows us how Jesus wished us always to approach His Gospel, to meditate on His work, to understand His purpose. It is not meant to be regarded by itself, as isolated from the rest of His teaching. It is not a lonely gem; it is a mirror which Christ's own hand holds up to reflect for us the essence of His message and its meaning. A little glass may reflect a great stretch of sky. As a summary of His aims and of His works and His prayers for mankind it is more authoritative than any précis or formulation which may be drawn up by men. It is from our Lord's own lips. It is expressly given not as one prayer among others, not as perhaps the best of many, but (what is much more) as typical, as showing forth that mental attitude to the Gospel which the believer is to assume in those most sacred moments when, in Christ's name, he approaches God in meditation and prayer. Here the wisdom of the Lord Himself has gathered together and set in order the major thoughts which He wishes Christians ever to keep in mind as characteristic of His work for mankind. These are the great things to pray for if we would follow the express direction of the Lord, and the order in which He names them shows the proportion and the emphasis which He wishes to be observed.

These are the essential matters in which men are to ask for God's help. Assuredly men have no right to seek this help unless they themselves earnestly desire and work for these things. Therefore this pattern prayer offers a very clear implied direction as to the principal things for which the Christian is here on earth to labour and which he is to make his prime practical objectives. If he faithfully follows the line of thought and action so strongly marked out here by Christ, he will be sure he is fulfilling the purposes of his Lord.

In its substance and in its proportions the Prayer of Jesus is parallel to the Ten Commandments of Moses. Both Prayer and Commandments divide into two parts; they are in the same order. The first deals with divine things; the second with human things. The first sets forth the honour and glory of God; the second, the needs and duties of man. But the Prayer belongs to a much more advanced stage in the spiritual evolution of mankind. The vista of social change and betterment opened in the Prayer is far more definite and more bright than anything in the earlier teaching. Christ, speaking from that point of view which he always maintained, the point of view of God and His heaven, indicated the prospect of the unification of mankind through their communion in a single spiritual ideal, their subjection to a single spiritual King, their obedience to one and the same universal law. Nineteen hundred years ago Jesus foreshadowed that very problem which circumstances have forced upon modern attention, defined the right approach to its solution, dealt with its spiritual aspects at large in his general teaching and drew the main primary thoughts together in a few pregnant phrases that His followers might have the central task of His Dispensation full in front of their minds whenever they said their prayers. He taught men to look forward to a wonderful change, a complete transformation in the condition of mankind that God's power, answering man's prayers, would produce. Something which He called the Kingdom of the Father would come down on earth, and the sovereign will of God would be accepted the world over as the rule of action.

This reorientation of social life was not to be entirely new; it was to be modelled after the pattern of life in heaven, as a sculptor might mould a piece of clay to the shape of a given figure. The ways of heaven are the original; the ways of earth are to be brought into correspondence, and mortals are to study and adopt the ideals of heaven in order to reproduce them in this lower world.

The emphasis of the Lord's Prayer confirms what the whole Gospel makes more than clear, that Christ's main objective was not mystical nor metaphysical nor doctrinal: on the contrary it was social and practical. He came to earth and lived and died, that he might open before all men the path to a diviner civilisation, might lift human life to a new level of knowledge and well-being.

No one can be unmoved by the impassioned spirituality of all that Christ said; but He never suggested that spirituality and ordinary human existence do not go together. Spirituality, on the contrary, is aided by progress in education and in civilisation. On the other hand, no progress can be maintained, and no true progress can be made, without the exertion of spiritual strength and energy.

He did not at all condemn earth-life nor deplore its existence nor minimise its importance. Far from it. There is not a hint of any kind of pessimism in His outlook. There is nothing in His utterances to correspond with such despairing denunciations as that of the great poet, who was so saddened by the human misery and wickedness about him that He cried out against man's birth as eclipsing the beauty of a world which God otherwise had made so lovely. He does not lament, nor encourage others to lament, the gathering of the shadows of mortality around human life as the years of childhood pass away. He proclaimed man's life on earth as a glorious privilege, an opportunity of winning an unending and unimaginable blessedness. He sought in every way, by precept and example, to impress on all the religious importance of social health and happiness. His purpose was to show men how to get the maximum of good results from their life on earth. The announcement of the herald angels had been Peace on Earth. One of Jesus' great prophecies was that the Meek shall inherit the Earth, meaning those who, like Moses and himself, had surrendered their wills to the will of God. He did not teach His disciples to pray that they might go to heaven when they died, but that they might do God's will on earth while they lived. God long ago had made the earth and everything and everybody in it and had seen that all was good; and now He so loved all the inhabitants of the earth that He sent His Son to teach and uplift them and be as one of themselves. There was nothing of the recluse nor of the ascetic about Jesus. He himself drew attention to this fact. The Baptist was bred in the wilderness and preached in the wilds, he dressed in the roughest garments and fed on the coarsest food; he was a lonely figure, and the burden of his eloquence was denunciatory. The contrast between him and Jesus was evident and striking; and the reason for it was hardly less evident. John's special task was to prepare men's hearts for the advent of the Messiah. He had to destroy the old corruptions and perversions, to break the mental idols set up by men, to warn, to condemn, to purify. He had to clear a highway for the approach of the Lord; and that highway was within the hearts of men. He did not attempt to reveal a system of new truth, as Jesus did later. His one positive pronouncement was the immediate Advent of Christ. Outside of this proclamation, the rest of his teaching was a rebuke and a call to repentance.

But Jesus, on the contrary, combined the closest communion with God with constant social intercourse. He moved as a man among men. He drew crowds about Him and welcomed them. He kept His disciples continually by Him. He was criticised because He shared men's feasts as well as their prayers, and mingled with people of all classes, not refusing His company even to outcasts—'a gluttonous man, and a winebibber', they cavilled, 'a friend of publicans and sinners'. He exemplified all that was best and most charming in social accessibility. He insisted on the social virtues—compassion, goodwill, forgiveness, charity, justice. He rebuked the Pharisees for their social iniquities and oppression of the poor—for devouring widows' houses and laying on others burdens which they would not touch with a finger themselves. He showed the Rich Man condemned after death to torment for no other reason than callous self-indulgence and neglect of the beggar who lay, day after day, helpless and in pain at his gate. The questions which He said the Divine Judge would ask of men at the Great Assize did not, in one instance, concern questions of orthodoxy or belief, but concerned only men's practical conduct to one another and especially to those in need. He heightened the moral standard of behaviour set by Moses, and in order to lift civilisation to a higher level, He introduced new social ordinances at the peril of His life. It was not so much on account of His purely spiritual revelation concerning the kingdom of heaven, eternal life and the like, that He incurred the hatred of the Scribes and Pharisees, as on account of His interference with the temporal regulations of Moses on such matters as divorce and the keeping of the Sabbath. How great must have been the importance He attached to social laws and customs, if for their sake He would defy the powerful classes and hasten His own destruction!

Destitute as He was, a wandering teacher without a place to lay His head at night, He started among His companions a benevolent fund and dispensed charity to those who were as poor as He.

He showed that every single human being was loved and cared for by God; He strongly insisted on every man's direct personal responsibility for his acts; but He never treated the individual as an isolated unit, but always and essentially as a member of society. No man could live to himself; he must live in relation to others. People in those days, much as to-day, divided all human society into two parts: their own fellow-countrymen and foreigners. The Jew put the Gentile in a different class from himself; as the Greek or Roman did with the 'barbarian'. The Baptist, preparing the minds of his listeners for the broader teaching of Jesus, had warned the Jews not to trust to their special privileges, nor to think that their being inheritors of the Promise would be enough to satisfy the approaching Messiah. '. . . begin not to say within yourselves, We have Abraham to our father: for I say unto you, that God is able of these stones to raise up children unto Abraham.' (Luke iii. 8.)

Jesus from the first refused to countenance the prejudice against a foreigner, and went even further than John. He proclaimed that all men are equal in the sight of God and are to be henceforth equal in the sight of one another. His first sermon, as recorded in Luke iv, was directed against the national and religious exclusiveness of the Jew, and He quoted in His support the incident of Elias and the widow of Sidon, and that of the cleansing of Naaman, the Syrian, from his leprosy. The immediate result of this address on the congregation was that 'all they in the synagogue, when they heard these things, were filled with wrath, And rose up, and thrust him out of the city, and led him unto the brow of the hill whereon their city was built, that they might cast him down headlong. But he passing through the midst of them went his way.' (Luke iv. 28–30.)

In the Parable of the Good Samaritan, He taught that in the New Dispensation the duty of being kind to a neighbour meant the duty of answering the need of every human being within reach, regardless of any difference in race, religion, tradition or any such thing. Spiritual kinship overbridged any such boundaries as these. His Gospel was to be preached to all nations indifferently;

and it must be carried to the uttermost ends of the globe before the next great step in world-evolution could be taken. To the Christian, as there was but one God and one heaven, so there was but one earth, a single home for the upbringing of all the Father's spiritual children. All human beings everywhere were to be regarded as members of one and the same universal spiritual society. In one of His comparisons, He likened them to sheep who, He said, would one day become one flock. He went even farther than this, and spoke of believers as being united in a way like that of the branches of a single tree, He himself being the central trunk from which all sprang and through which they all were joined to one another. The world-unity which He had in view was not outward nor of a superficial kind: it was very real and deep-seated. It was an inner unity of thought and feeling, of outlook on life, of spiritual experience and knowledge. He said very little about organisation and He postponed questions of world-government. He dealt with the first things.

It was always His insistence that the unification of the human race was a matter to be proceeded to by steps and degrees. There were certain measures which must be taken in hand first, and others second. It was not for man to determine the order of these steps; it was for God. The right and proper order had long ago been established by divine law; and man's part was to discover and follow the provisions of this law. If man preferred his own way to the way laid out by the principles of evolution, good results could not be obtained; there must of necessity be delays and disappointment. Christ defined with the utmost clearness and emphasis what was the order of progress; man must, under the law of the universe, seek first the kingdom of God and God's righteousness: he must before all else in his heart hallow God's name. Other things must come second and would follow if the first forward step were rightly taken.

So direct, so strong, so telling was Christ's attack upon every kind of divisive prejudice and pride, that He paid for His teaching the price of His life, and showed Himself very ready to sacrifice Himself in the cause of truth and unification. All His commandments, negative and positive, were such as to put an end to estrangement and to promote affection, harmony and concord. He sought in every way to cleanse men's hearts of selfishness and to educate them from self-centredness to world-centredness. Love is the first commandment. Love is the second commandment. There is no third commandment. Turn in the New Testament where one will, the counsels of Christ are all in the direction of one effect, one end: amity, fellowship, unity. To glance over the Sermon on the Mount is to see that Christ there blesses the merciful and the peacemakers; He bids men be reconciled with one another before they come to worship God; He denounces anger and enjoins truthfulness; He commends forbearance and generosity and a goodwill that has no thought of reciprocity: a man is to do to others as he would have them do to him, and whatever they do to him (be it as bad as it may) he is to be as kind to them as he can, to help them, bless them and pray for them.

So important did He think the duty of forgiveness that He included it in the Lord's Prayer and made a man's forgiveness of his brethren the measure of the forgiveness he might expect from God. So strongly did Christians long ago realise the importance of the need and the duty of forgiveness that they introduced their hope of God's forgiveness of their sins into the Apostles' Creed.

Christ revealed nothing about the organisation of a system of international law. He did not take, in Isaiah's phrase, 'the government . . . upon his shoulder'. (Isa. ix. 6.) He did not define any social pattern of world-order. Such a problem did not arise. The earth at that time had not been explored. No one's imagination then could picture all the empires and peoples of the planet as unified into a single co-ordinated system, as forming some kind of universal theocracy. Mankind was altogether too immature to develop those powers of heart and soul which would be needed for so great a feat of co-operation. It was as yet too inexperienced in the arts of government. Jesus' mission was spiritual only. It dealt with men as men, as units of the Kingdom to be, and brought them individually a new degree of consciousness, which, when spread from heart to heart through the world, would enable them to face the further and higher tasks involved in reconstituting the whole social order of the planet.

The union of all mankind at which Christ aimed was not a mere brotherhood. Men were not only to become like one flock but at the same time they were to have one shepherd. Believers were not to be as so many dismembered boughs of a tree, but were to be boughs living and growing on one trunk. The world-ideal which Christ sought to realise is given most commonly in the figure of a family. All men were indeed brothers; but the primary fact was they were sons, sons of one Father. God was to be conceived of as Father; the apostles prayed to him as Abba, Father; every Christian was instructed to pray to him as Father; Christ's own particular title, Son of God, reminded every believer of the Heavenly Father. Whenever one prayed, one's first thought was always to be of reverence for the Father and for all that was of the Father.

So vigorously did Christ urge upon men this remembrance of a unifying Fatherhood that He bade men call no man on earth father; they had only one Creator, the Father in heaven; and instead of thinking of their human fathers on earth, through whom they were divided into many families, they were to acknowledge as a reality only one true Fatherhood, that of the One Universal God, the Maker of all, Who loved all and watched over all and provided for all.

If they would make a steadfast effort and develop within themselves that deep spiritual love with which Christ endowed them, the earth verily would become one home and all the members of the human race one family.

CHAPTER XI

THE REJECTION BY THE MEN OF EARTH

Jesus did not bring His Revelation to a people whose minds were open, who loved truth for truth's sake and were ready to welcome it from whatever quarter it came. On the contrary, He brought it to a people lifted up with the most extravagant pride of religion and of race, who believed themselves the favourites and confidants of God and who were led by a group of divines that preyed on the fanatical prejudices of the laity.

Circumstances more uncongenial for the presentation of a new, a progressive and a highly spiritual Revelation could hardly be imagined. One might almost think it would have been easier to proclaim the Gospel in Rome itself, the capital of the Western world, where men were tolerant and interested in Eastern philosophies, and where there was no organised hierarchy nor closed system of orthodoxy to idealise human tradition and stifle thought.

Rome, however, had no first claim to the New Teaching, nor had any land other than Palestine. The New Revelation was a continuation of the Old Revelation given by Moses. To the Jews alone belonged the sublime and awful privilege of first receiving it; and to them belonged too the responsibility of using their great privilege aright. The Gospel could not be understood save as the fulfilment of the prophecies and promises recorded in the Old Testament, and in particular in its relation to the work of Mosaism. This connexion was a vital part of the Message itself, linking it with the eternity of God and His redemptive love. Because of it, the Gospel in a special sense belonged to the Jews, and was, so to speak, an indigenous product in the Holy Land. Yet by a strange and tragic irony it was this very connexion which blinded the Jews to the truth of the New Teaching and which caused the divines to denounce and martyr their Messiah.

The goodness and charm of Jesus have captivated and held the imaginations of men for centuries; sceptics, if they deny His claims in their fullness, admit with readiness the ideal beauty of His life, of His character and of His teaching; history has made evident the reality of His power over men, and there has seldom been a time when men, conscious of their unworthiness, have looked towards Him with a greater longing than now. We are altogether at a loss to understand the dullness of the Jews in refusing to pay Him honour; and we cannot express our bewilderment at their associating His name with that of Beelzebub and their procuring His crucifixion as a public enemy.

We may dismiss the matter, supposing perhaps that they, in spite of their zeal for God and for Moses and their loyalty and generosity towards their church, were persons of unparalleled depravity and their action was due to some fatality.

But the Jewish divines and the multitudes were not alone in their lack of faith. The disciples themselves were slow of understanding, feeble in faith, prone to doubt. Their actions show this abundantly. Jesus said so expressly. Their lack of faith astonished Him, wearied Him; He used to rebuke them for it and for their doubts; their faith was not as big as a mustard seed; conscious of their infirmity they prayed Him rather helplessly to increase their faith for them.

The divines, indeed, martyred Jesus and destroyed their nation; the disciples confessed Him, served Him and through them Christ's saving Message was carried to mankind. But the difference between the two was not that between jet black and purest white, between no faith at all and perfection of faith. The disciples, too, had their spiritual temptations and difficulties, which some of them overcame more fully than did others; they were not quick to apprehend the bearing or the essence of the new revelation. If their glorious record shows nothing whatever of that cruel envy which blighted the Pharisee and the Scribe, yet the disciples shared the narrowing prejudices of every orthodox Jew. That which in this respect distinguished the disciple from the divine was that the divine surrendered abjectly to his prejudices, while the disciples struggled and persevered and conquered, and through their conquest attained the vision of God and became messengers of His truth.

'Blessed are the poor,' said Jesus in his ordination address. The disciples who stood before Him proved the truth of His statement; for it was the privileges and the leadership of the Scribes and Pharisees that made more difficult for them the independence of mind which the disciples, 'babes' as they were, abundantly evinced.

If they were as 'babes', yet the most serious and formidable problem which confronted the disciples was in its nature intellectual. It was not a sin of the flesh but a sin of the mind which ruined the Scribes and Pharisees and wrecked the Jewish nation. The harlots and sinners and publicans and outcasts found easier access to Jesus than did those afflicted with pride of caste and intellect. The great difficulty that beset every conforming Mosaist was that of setting the New Message of Christ in its right relation to the Message of the older Dispensation. The Scribes and Pharisees utterly failed to surmount this obstacle: they did not even try. The disciples succeeded, but only after much delay and many mistakes. If we, with another tradition and at this distance of time, are to understand the frame of mind of the first-century Jew and to appreciate his dilemma, we shall need imagination and dramatic sympathy. The point of view from which the modern Christian naturally looks on the life and the teaching and the surroundings of Jesus of Nazareth is wholly different from that of Jesus' compatriots. We look back across nineteen centuries of Christian civilisation and see its lowly founder illuminated by the glory of his posthumous achievement. We know the Gospel as the Magna Charta of the West, and as more. We see it stand in independent and dominating splendour. When we open our Bibles, that to which our hearts and minds first turn is the New Revelation. The Gospel of the Lord Christ stands in full view, filling the foreground of our thoughts. Behind it in a distant perspective, we descry the cruder preparatory teaching of Judaism out of which Christianity arose. But the Israelite who listened to Jesus was nursed in a religious tradition more than two thousand years old, which he cherished as the one hope and glory of his nation and of himself; while the Christian Faith existed only in its pure essence and its germ, and the great system with which we are familiar had not begun to take shape even in imagination.

To us, the two major problems of Christianity are its influence on life and on civilisation, and secondly, its extension throughout the earth. But in the New Testament there was a third major problem which has now no practical meaning and little interest, but which, in that age, was of vital and urgent importance. It was the problem of development, of transition, of passing over from Mosaism to Christianity and of making between the two systems the right connexion.

We may regard with cold eyes the flowering of Judaism into Christianity and scrutinise it as a matter of history, as a process of intellectual development. But in its own day it had another appearance. The New Testament with its warm humanity and faithful realism shows that to the disciples and other Jewish Christians the transition was a cause of inward stress and mystical struggle, a cause of heart-searchings and heart-burnings, a cause of difference of opinion and sharp division. If we think of that transition as an issue long past and now dead, we ignore the strong testimony of the Gospel-narrative. Around this issue gathers much that is darkest in the misunderstandings, the mistakes, the failures, the tragedies, the crimes of the story. To it may be traced the blindness of the Jewish divines, their rejection and their crucifixion of their Lord.

It has more than an historical—it has, too, a profound psychological and religious interest, and its significance still lives. Their failure was due to a mistake to which, in principle, human nature is always open—the mistake of confusing what is accidental in religion with what is essential, what is formal with what is vital. They did not understand—perhaps they chose not to understand—that religion is a living, growing force and that God's method of revelation is continuous and progressive. Their history shows in a manner as realistic and dramatic as can well be imagined how spiritual bigotry and ignorance may weaken and deprave the human soul, and with unseen hands produce inexorably the most momentous changes in the fate of men and of nations. The Israelites were in religion a self-opinionated and highly exclusive people. This characteristic marked them out not only when they were in their own land among their own kind, but also when they travelled and dwelt in foreign parts. Roman writers such as Tacitus (*Hist.* v. 5) and Juvenal (*Sat.* 14, 103) advert to it. They had their own fixed and immovable ideas about Mosaism. They venerated all Scripture as verbally inspired. They took it in the most literal sense. For its greater protection, they had enclosed it within an elaborate system of Traditions which had been deduced from Scripture or were thought either to be implied in it or to be needed for its amplification. These traditions of the Elders were as sacred as the Word of God itself. They were fixed and unchangeable. Divine knowledge consisted in knowing them, and righteousness in keeping them. None could expound either Holy Writ or Tradition authoritatively save the Scribes; and whatever the Scribe said on any question must be and always was the last word, the express truth.

These views were not confined to men such as Caiaphas and Simon the Pharisee and Gamaliel and Nicodemus, but were the common property of all orthodox Israelites, both those who believed in Jesus and those who did not.

Amongst those who confessed their faith in Christ, not the least ardent in their churchmanship were the two leaders who figure so prominently in the New Testament —Paul and Peter: Paul who described himself as 'a Pharisee, a son of Pharisees', who wrote: 'Did God cast off his people? God forbid. For I also am an Israelite' (Romans xi. 1); who loved his fellow-Israelites to the end and said of them: Theirs 'is the adoption, and the glory, and the covenants, and the giving of the law, and the service *of God* and the promises; (theirs) are the fathers, (theirs) is Christ as concerning the flesh, who is over all, God blessed for ever.' (Romans ix. 4–5.) Paul, whose interpretations of Christianity are so coloured with Judaism that sometimes one can hardly understand his allusions or his argument without some knowledge of rabbinical lore—and Peter, who clung to outworn Mosaic customs with an unreasoning obstinacy that called down a just rebuke from Paul.

Every good Jew, whether a cleric or a layman, whether he came from Judæa or Galilee, believed in the finality of Moses' Revelation and in the everlasting permanence of all the Mosaic rites, customs, sacrifices and laws. He believed that his people were the elect of God among all nations, that the Scribes were the only teachers of true religion in the world, and that the Messiah when he came would reduce the Gentiles to their proper position of subordination and establish for ever the sovereignty of the Jewish people and their theocratic system.

When Jesus appeared and announced that the Revelation of Moses was not final, that its moral precepts were not exhaustive nor the highest possible; that the secular and ecclesiastical laws of Mosaism were subject to modification and to repeal; when He announced that the appointed time for these changes and for a new Independent Revelation had come, He challenged the accepted view and the established belief of every Israelite who heard Him. If a Jew were in his heart more interested in the observances of his traditional religion than in its spirit, he would view the new teaching with little comprehension and with much distaste; if these observances were the chief occupation of his life, he would view it with fear and hate.

The young prophet from Nazareth was indeed asking of His auditors a great deal. He was asking them to give up usages and customs, ways of thought and habits of belief which had been honoured among them for centuries and which had become firmly entrenched in the hearts and the lives of all. He called upon them to trust themselves, soul, spirit, and body too, to the new teaching of one who offered them no recognised human credentials whatever.

The crisis was indeed a test of spiritual faith and of moral courage. It was meant to be so. It was designed to separate the true-hearted from the insincere, those who genuinely believed in God from those who played a game of make-believe. But Jesus was not demanding of his generation the impossible. He was not trying the Israelites beyond their strength nor seeking to exact from them more than they could give. The Jews were quite capable of recognising the New Revelation: their tragic refusal to do so was not inevitable, it was of their own free choice. Who will imagine that God would have sent His Son into the world with inadequate powers to achieve His purpose? Who will imagine that God condemned the Jews and punished them with an era-long exile and humiliation for an offence for which they were not truly responsible?

The fact that their rejection of their Messiah was their own uncompelled, free act was in so many words affirmed by Jesus when he said:

> O Jerusalem, Jerusalem, *thou* that killest the prophets, and stonest them which are sent unto thee, how often would I have gathered thy children together, even as a hen gathereth her chickens under *her* wings, and ye would not! Behold, your house is left unto you desolate. (Matt. xxiii. 37–38.)

Had the divines of the day consented to examine dispassionately the new doctrine, they soon would have found proof of its authenticity. But they refused. Prejudice, envy, love of leadership, closed their minds. So soon as they perceived that their privileges were threatened, they hugged their exclusiveness tighter than before, and their fear roused them to hatred and cruelty.

The same emergency that showed up the falsity of the Scribes and Pharisees brought to light the sincerity and true-heartedness of the apostles. Their faith may have been weak, their understanding not great: but they chose to follow Christ. They struggled against their infirmities; if they wandered into error they turned back into the way of truth. By slow degrees they were put by their patient Master through the difficult lessons they had to master. They learned that this man whom they loved and trusted was the Messiah: they learned that He was a spiritual Messiah, and finally they learned that He was independent of Mosaism and brought with Him a new law and a new book.

CHAPTER XII

THE FOUNDING OF A CHRISTIAN COMMUNITY

The manner of teaching which Jesus employed in dealing with the Jewish people and in particular with the apostles is one of the most interesting among the minor features of His Revelation. It was not a method calculated to give the most sensational or the quickest results. It was one which would proceed little by little and would of necessity take time. One observes, on reflection, that the method was in reality an application on a small scale to the individual mind of the self-same principle which the Eternal Lord of Evolution uses on a large scale in the education of the soul of mankind.

Jesus neither had nor desired human credentials. His Five Witnesses are given in the fifth chapter of St. John: the Baptist—His own life and teaching—the Father—Holy Scripture—and Moses. Jonah had one sign to give to the Ninevites—his inspired message of God's compassion: Jesus likewise (so He taught) had His sign, which was His divine Message; and that sign must suffice, for He would give no more. In accordance with the determination He had made before the beginning of His ministry, He did not attempt to force anyone's conversion or hurry anyone's enlightenment by resorting to supernatural means. He would not suppress incredulity by doing wonders nor exemplify His Messianic power by physical miracles. When He was importuned to confirm His utterances by performing some prodigious feat, He refused. A portent, had He consented to give one, would have produced no constructive effect on people's minds; it would have made the wrong appeal: it would not have awakened spiritual faith nor promoted that most delicate process of soul-development. In the parable of the Rich Man and Lazarus, Jesus quoted Abraham, in paradise, as saying that if men on earth were not persuaded by the teaching of Moses and of the prophets, they would not be persuaded even by one who came back from the dead to warn them.

He would heal a sick man, not to display His power, but out of pure kindness and compassion; He would strictly enjoin him to tell no one about the incident. Ostentation, even in what might appear the best cause, was not within His plan. He would raise the dead, for was He not the Prince of Life, and had He not come to give men a more abundant life—was He not Himself the Resurrection, so that any one who believed in Him had eternal life and was for ever immune from death? After-ages and more materialistic minds might reduce His miracles of life-giving and represent Him as merely restoring to dead men the physical life which had been taken from them and which must soon be taken again from them—this time beyond recovery. Such restoration would indeed spread amazement and consternation far and wide, beyond the borders of Palestine, and no doubt as far as Rome itself and put every Scribe, Pharisee and sceptic to shame and to silence. But the true miracles of life-giving which Jesus performed and which assuredly proved beyond any doubt His Messiahship were spiritual miracles wrought upon men's hearts and souls, which the carnal ego could not see nor the mundane mind appreciate, and which for that reason might be well symbolised by parables of men called back from beyond the grave.

Jesus, in fine, showed in every way the utmost deference to man's independent will. He offered to men truth as a gift. He did not urge it upon them, not even upon the disciples; He did not beg them to accept it, nor try by any strategem to induce them to believe in it. With care and infinite patience, He measured His teaching to the capacity of those whom He taught, and as their receptivity improved, He gave them a little more and again a little more.

It is in His education of the Twelve whom He chose to be continually with Him that the progressiveness of His teaching is brought out most clearly and most dramatically. He did not attempt to suggest to the disciples at once, or quickly, all that He intended them to learn from Him. He, of course, well knew (as we with wisdom of the event know too) that He was about to institute such colossal changes in human history and human character as no Hebrew in the past, not Moses or Abraham himself had contemplated. He would soon lay upon the apostles one of the most tremendous responsibilities ever undertaken by human beings. But He did not try to explain to them what that responsibility would be nor how great would be the civilisation which He was about to found through their agency. They were quite unprepared for such knowledge and quite incapable of penetrating His meaning or visualising future developments. He told them very little about their future work. His endeavour was so to strengthen them that they would be fit for the emergency when it arose. He taught with the purpose of opening their hearts, quickening their faith, intensifying their spirituality, so as to equip them for the responsibilities all too soon to be laid upon them. At first He told them little in plain, explicit language, and He chose the subjects of His teaching less with a view to satisfying their curiosity than with a view to remedying their moral deficiencies and to converting weakness into strength. His aim was evidently not merely to change the views of the apostles, but (what was much more difficult) so to change their hearts and minds that their views would then change themselves. He once said that whatever a man found to do he should do with his might; and assuredly His teaching was thorough. There was something in His utterance, however undogmatic or serene His manner, which made His words sink deep. He breathed about those who were with Him a spiritual atmosphere in which superstitions and follies weakened and withered. He did not try to blot out of the disciples' minds the whole system of a former belief that He might build a new and better system in its place. On the contrary. He sought to disturb their religion as little as possible, to encourage the growth of whatever was good in it and to let whatever was corrupt die through its own unsoundness. It was not by imparting items of information to them that He sought to guide them to a knowledge of God; rather He sought to invigorate their minds and strengthen their intuitions that they might of themselves learn more of the divine truth which was being shed upon them. Through this method, undazzling and unrhetorical as it was, Jesus was able to recreate and regenerate the souls of the apostles and lead them gradually onward and upward from their original ignorance and infirmity to the heights of wisdom and power which ultimately they attained.

The basic fact on which the New Era and its civilisation were to be built was the fact of Jesus' Messiahship. But Jesus was in no hurry to announce this even to the disciples. His wish was so to increase their spirituality that they would be enabled to discover it for themselves; for their appreciation of the truth would, in that case, be more full and more firm than if He spared them the effort and told them with His own lips.

For this reason Jesus refused to be drawn into any premature declaration of His identity. Two attempts to draw from Him a clear statement of His status are recorded, one friendly and one unfriendly: both times He refused. The Baptist from prison had sent messengers to Jesus to ask, 'Art thou he that should come, or do we look for another?' (Matt. xi. 3.) The Baptist, of course, himself well knew that Jesus was the Messiah, but he wished that others should know. He felt his own end approaching, and he hoped that before the Herald was put to silence in the grave the Lord whose advent he had proclaimed would see fit to declare Himself publicly to the world. He determined that before he died he would give Christ at least an opportunity and an invitation to make the great pronouncement. Jesus gave an answer which implied but did not openly state that He was indeed the Christ and was doing the Christ's work; and (Matt. xi. 4–5) was healing the spiritually sick, giving spiritual knowledge to the ignorant, bestowing eternal life on those buried in mortality: and 'blessed is *he*, whosoever shall not be offended in me' (Matt. xi. 6), meaning, blessed were those who, in spite of the personal simplicity and lowliness of Jesus, were spiritual enough to discern His heavenly power and His divine dignity.

At a later date, shortly before the end of His life, the chief priests and the scribes and the elders assembled, and approaching Jesus as He taught in the temple, sought from Him such a definite declaration of His claims as they hoped soon to be able to use against Him with deadly effect. 'By what authority', they enquired, 'doest thou these things? and who gave thee this authority?' Jesus courteously replied that He would answer them if they first would answer a question of His; and He asked them, whence came the authority of John the Baptist? When they could not tell Him, He said, 'Neither tell I you by what authority I do these things.' (Matt. xxi. 23–27; *see also* Mark xi. 28–33.)

The people at large, like the disciples, were attracted by Jesus, they gathered about Him, they hung upon His words, they were charmed by His sweetness and astonished at the strange power that was in His words; but like the apostles, they did not realise He was the long-expected Messiah. The divines had deduced from a number of Old Testament texts what the Messiah would be like and what He would do. He would be something like what they imagined Moses and Joshua had been, a great warrior-deliverer, and He would carry the work of Jewish emancipation which these two leaders had begun to a still more glorious and resounding conclusion. Moses had given the Israelites the Holy Land: the Messiah would give them the world. Of all this the divines were quite satisfied, and of a great deal more, and they had for generations been telling the Jews in school and synagogue what great things this mighty earth-conqueror would do for them as soon as he made his appearance. Jesus of Nazareth did not at all resemble this Messiah: He had no throne, no sword and was a simple, poor man. Some people were so deeply impressed by His doctrine and personality they thought He was like an Old Testament prophet; no one thought He was the Messiah. Even the disciples themselves for a time did not think so. They loved Him; they regarded Him with wonder and awe; they felt and often spoke as if they were children before Him, He was so wise and so great; they were ready to leave their homes to be with Him and to learn from Him; they believed they would follow Him anywhere. Yet He did not seem to them like a Messiah. The Messiah would be quite a different sort of person. They would recognise Him at once because the Scribes had drawn such a vivid picture of Him, and it was the Scribes' business to know all about such matters. Jesus did not conceal His identity from them; but on the other hand He did not hasten to proclaim it. He was content for a while to imply it. In the Sermon on the Mount He made statements of Himself which could only be true of a Messiah, and of a great Messiah. But He did not affirm in so many words His true dignity. He taught His disciples and encouraged them and led them with Him into such a strange, new, beautiful world of spiritual values that, by degrees, they became able to appreciate something of His true majesty and splendour. There began to dawn on them the truth this radiant Being was in reality more than they had suspected at first. Weeks passed; and months: still Jesus did not open to them the great mystery. He watched, and continued His training of them till He saw that, at last, the moment had come: they had reached, or some of them had reached, the very edge of the great recognition.

The experience of the disciples, therefore, was in contrast to that of Simeon and of the prophetess Anna recorded in the second chapter of St. Luke. The intuition of these two aged people perceived at once the identity of the infant as the Promised One; but they did not live to learn in what a strange and unexpected manner the child would become the glory of Israel and shed light upon the Gentiles.

The account given in St. John's Gospel puts the acknowledgment that Jesus is the Christ, the Messiah, the Son of God, together with the changing of Simon's name to Peter, at the very beginning of the ministry; in fact, before the actual call of any of the disciples. But St. John assuredly does not intend here to contradict the chronology of St. Matthew, which Christendom has always accepted. Rather, according to the spirit and the purpose of his unique Gospel, these words, like many other words in other connexions, must be taken in some profound mystical sense or as having an important theological rather than historical meaning. But even when Jesus saw that the first stage of His preparation of the disciples was complete and that the right moment had come to make known to them His station as the Christ, He did not then declare His identity to them with His own lips.

He did not, in fact, ever make an open declaration (according to the first three Gospels) until his trial. Then in answer to a direct question from the High Priest, he gives (to His own destruction) the great claim which they had vainly sought to establish from the mouth of witnesses: nobody could be found who had actually heard Jesus assert that He was the Messiah. (Matt. xxvi. 63–64.)

It was from the lips of Peter that there came the first declaration of Jesus' Messiahship ever made on this earth; and Jesus drew the pronouncement from him. At a time chosen by Himself, Jesus brought forward the problem of who He really was and who the Jewish public said He was. The disciples told Him that some supposed He was John the Baptist miraculously come back from the dead, some that He was Elijah, or else Jeremiah or some other prophet. They said no more; they did not volunteer what they thought of these opinions nor did they give their own opinion. Jesus propounded them a further question: 'But who say ye that I am?' (Matt. xvi. 15.) The disciples' reply came from St. Peter: 'Thou art the Christ, the Son of the living God.' Jesus at once accepted the title and pronounced on Peter the only personal blessing of a disciple quoted in the four gospels: 'Blessed art thou, Simon Bar-jona: for flesh and blood hath not revealed *it* unto thee, but my Father which is in heaven . . .'

Jesus left no doubt in the minds of those present of the immense significance of this pronouncement. Peter, in virtue of his confession and of his brilliant vision of the truth, was declared the first believer, the first Christian. Hereafter there would arise down the ages others who would share his intuition, who instead of reflecting the belief of those about them, instead of owing their faith to tradition, would, like Peter, receive not from their fellow-men but immediately from the Father Himself an inward understanding of Christ's nature and message. As the first Christian, so should be other Christians: they would be distinguished from others as Peter was distinguished from others. They would have from God an independent realisation in their own hearts of the Messiahship of Christ.

They would be knit with Peter, the First Christian, by this common experience; and out of all such believers (their hearts indissolubly united together in love for God and Christ) would be built Christ's true congregation into which all who entered were admitted not by their fellow-men, not by flesh and blood, but directly by the Father in heaven Himself.

To such Christians Jesus committed the evangelisation of mankind and all the authority and discipline which would be needed for the prosecution of the task. So long as He lived, all power was His; but He foresaw that soon He would be taken from them and He now began to prepare them for their heavy responsibility. The time would come (and come at no distant date) when the burden would be shifted from His shoulders and would be laid on theirs. The spiritual future of mankind would depend on them and on those who after them would walk in their steps—the steps, that is, of humble faith and of intuitive assurance of the reality of their Master's Messianic title. However lowly or obscure or poor such followers might be, however overwhelming the opposition marshalled against them, Jesus promised that no power on earth or under the earth ever should prevail against them. Nothing could refute their witness. They and such as they were the true servants of human progress, the children of spiritual evolution, the destined inheritors of the earth.

This appointment of the Twelve to 'bind' and 'loose' implied the revocation of all authority given under the Mosaic Dispensation. Officials of the Jewish Church would no longer be in the line of spiritual evolution nor empowered to work as agents of a Dispensation to promote the spiritual progress of mankind. The authority of the Kingdom was to be transferred henceforth to the Christians.

The removal of the Scribes from their position as teachers must have saddened the heart of Jesus. It was called for, it was forced upon Him by their own arrogance and craving for personal leadership. Had they really had the divine wisdom they pretended to have, they would have been the first to acclaim their Messiah and would have retained the leadership (or rather become the divine servants) of the people. Their spiritual influence would have spread far and wide among the nations and they would have won eternal, and perhaps also temporal, fame and glory. Often and often God would have gathered them under the wings of His love and saved them from destruction; but they would not heed, and their house was made a desolation. (Matt. xxiii. 37–38.)

This confession of Jesus as the Christ, the Son of the living God, and His acceptance of the title, mark a central and crucial point in the spiritual education of the Twelve.

At first there was a doubt. The disciples remembered the prophecy that Elijah would come before the Messiah, and Elijah, as far as they knew, had not yet come: how then could Jesus be the Christ of prophecy? Jesus explained that Elijah had indeed come and the Jews had done to him as they listed. The disciples knew that He referred to the Baptist and they began to see what none else saw, how in Jesus the prophecies of the Old Testament were being fulfilled before their eyes.

Realising now that their Master was none less than the Messiah, they became conscious of the importance of their own advancement and authority. As the chosen friends of the Messiah and His inner council, they would be made rulers in Israel as soon as the Messianic kingdom was set up. It was not long before they were disputing among themselves who should sit nearest the Throne and take precedence of the others and wield the greatest power over the people.

Jesus no doubt foresaw this development and He took pains quickly to disillusion them, to start them along the second part of their spiritual education and to discourage the rise of any such foolish and unworthy ambitions. He warned them in plain, strong words that a complete surprise awaited them; that He would not prove to be the kind of Messiah they had been led to expect: far, far otherwise. They would gain no praise from men for following Him: quite the contrary. He foretold that He must go to Jerusalem; and there in the Sacred City suffer many things at the hands of the very elect of His own people, the elders and chief priests and scribes, and be set at nought and mocked and crucified. But, He explained, no cross could kill His spirit, no grave could hold His power, no darkness dim His light.

This blunt and terrible warning, given designedly so soon after the declaration of His Messiahship, shocked and horrified the disciples. No doubt it was meant so to do. They could not believe it nor comprehend it. He was the Messiah. No defeat could happen to the Messiah, least of all in Jerusalem and at the hands of the leaders of the Chosen People.

Peter again became the apostles' spokesman and gave utterance to those unspiritual conceptions of Christhood in which all Jews had been trained and from which the disciples had not yet shaken loose.

Then Peter took him, and began to rebuke him, saying, Be it far from thee, Lord: this shall not be unto thee. (Matt. xvi. 22.)

Jesus instantly, in the sternest language possible, reprimanded Peter and repudiated his opinion as being of the essence of evil; and then, proceeding, set forth the law of self-sacrifice, and the certainty that in spite of His apparent defeat, He would in God's strength triumph over all opposition; His Cause would suffer eclipse for three days, but for no longer.

This new strange spiritual conception of the Messianic office bewildered the disciples. They did not, they would not reject it; they tried to accept it. But their minds were not flexible enough to grasp it. It sank into their hearts very, very slowly. In spite of their Master's vigorous and reiterated teaching, they could only abandon the familiar idea of the Messiah with toil and pain; they clung to it, as it were, in spite of themselves. Even at the end of Jesus' ministry, they had not been able to understand His meaning nor succeeded in their efforts to accept His statement as to His sufferings and His violent death. They still expected He would set up some form of external kingship in which they would enjoy positions of glory and power among men; and Jesus' last efforts in their spiritual education were directed to training them in the virtue of humility and in the ideal of service.

Before He could bring home to their hearts this difficult and unwelcome lesson, He was taken from them. The tragic close of His career brought their spiritual failure to unmistakable expression. Peter denied His Master thrice; Thomas doubted Him; Judas betrayed Him; all in the hour of His danger forsook Him and fled. The crucifixion cast them into utter amazement and despair. The whole mental fabric which their pride and imagination had built up was shattered in a moment and fallen. Their world was empty. Their beloved Lord was defeated—the mocking scribe was right. They had made some terrible mistake . . . For three days the Cause of Christ lay in their hearts dead and buried. None can tell what might have happened, had it not been for the intuition and courage of one who was not of their number—a woman, Mary of Magdala. She it was who was the first to understand the reality of Eternal Life and Christ's Eternal Sonship. She understood, before those to whom they were spoken, the words of Jesus after His rebuke of Peter.

> If any *man* will come after me, let him deny himself, and take up his cross, and follow me. For whosoever will save his life shall lose it: and whosoever will lose his life for my sake shall find it . . . the Son of man shall come in the glory of his Father with his angels . . . (Matt. xvi. 24–25, 27.)

Quicker than any of the Twelve, she perceived the reality of His kingship, and recognised that if His body was dead, His spirit was indestructible and was alive breathing in mortal power. She cheered the disciples. She communicated to them her vision, quickened their faith and renewed their courage. Purified by their suffering, animated by her spiritual power, they now perceived for the first time the incorporeal nature of the dominion and glory of their Lord and of His kingdom. Not till the first Easter was the great confession of an earlier day completed; and if the glory of that confession belongs to Peter the glory of making it in the fullness of its spiritual sense belongs to the Magdalene. But even at this stage in their mental growth, even after this appalling trial and this celestial illumination the disciples had not shaken off the hold of convention and superstition nor realised the independence of the Revelation of their Lord. They still clung to the idea that Christ had come to reform the Jewish church. As if to show how closely ingrained in their habit of mind were the old traditions and how slow and toilsome was their transition to a larger truth, the New Testament records that for years after the Resurrection Peter, the leader of the Twelve and the greatest of them, could not free himself from his old thraldom to Jewish custom—nor was he alone in his hyper-conservatism. The disciples might accept Jesus' abrogation of the law of the Sabbath and his prohibition of divorce, but they could not accept the principle on which these changes depended. They could not apply it to other parts of the Mosaic tradition. When Jesus was no longer with them in the flesh to give definite directions and rulings, their inclination was to hold fast to an old belief unless he had explicitly rejected it. In spite of such general remarks of Jesus as his statement that new wine would need new bottles, and a more specific remark such as that in Mark vii. 18 (Luke xi. 41) that what a man ate did not defile him, but what he thought ('*This he said*, making all meats clean'), Peter and others with him sincerely maintained that the observance of circumcision and of the distinction between clean and unclean meats was still called for under the Christian law. Nor even when with difficulty he changed his mind on this point and adopted a larger opinion, did he find it easy at first to adhere, under stress, to his new point of view. (Gal. ii.)

Whatever may be the psychological explanation of the extraordinary fact, it was Paul, the ex-Pharisee, the extremist, more thoroughly steeped in Scribal lore than any or all of the other early Christians, who made this mental transition from Judaism to Christianity more quickly, as well as more discerningly than any of his contemporaries, and showed the older believers how to apply to Mosaism the principles of religious development they had been taught by Christ. Doubtless, a philosophic temperament, eagerness of mind and intellectual courage, travel and variety of experience (he was not a Palestinian Jew) as well as the particular grace of God, helped him to this remarkable feat. But he did not achieve his faith without strong effort. Long before his conversion his heart had been torn by a struggle between old error and new truth. He resisted the call of God, and like many another great evangelist in after ages, like St. Patrick, for example, and like St. Xavier, he refused to surrender his proud independence till, at last, the force of truth overwhelmed him and he realised the enormity of refusing to confess his knowledge and to go forth to give battle for his dear Lord. 'For if I preach the gospel,' he cried, 'I have nothing to glory of; for necessity is laid upon me; for woe is unto me, if I preach not the gospel.' (I Cor. ix. 16.)

He, like Peter, was vouchsafed the privilege of an outward vision to strengthen him in his struggle. He needed a period of seclusion and meditation to win peace after the turmoil of conflict, and to think out the manifold problems that beset him. But once he became sure of himself and of his position, he went forward, never looking back. Owing to the tardiness of Peter and the other disciples, he took their place as the chief expounder and propagator of the Gospel. His point of view and his views (even when largely personal) have greatly influenced Christian interpretations up to the present time. He it was who, moved by the same intoxication of love for Jesus as the earlier disciples, was the first to recognise the comprehensiveness of Jesus' teaching, to see the significance of the command to gather all nations into the kingdom and to paint in clear outline the vision of a world-community bound into one by the inward bond of a common faith. He never met Jesus in the flesh, but he learned from Jesus' words and bore witness more clearly than any other of his time to the truth that man's freedom does not impair God's sovereignty, that world-history is radically a spiritual process, that the Creative Will laid out its course from the beginning and that mankind (one and all) tread haltingly and erringly a path ordained before the foundation of the world.

CHAPTER XIII

THE ANNOUNCEMENT OF THE KINGDOM OF GOD

Whatever obstacles were put in their way by the force of tradition or the pride of learning were overcome by the Apostles' love for Christ and their vision of His great purpose. He dwelt in their hearts and they longed to serve Him, to please Him, to walk in the path He had laid out for them, to give His Message and to impart the joy of knowing Him. This love which held them so fast to Jesus was a wholly new experience to them. They had been brought up in an atmosphere of reverence, accepting a religion which came to them by inheritance and which they had received without question and without ecstasy. But now through this association with Jesus they entered a new spiritual world. He poured on them a warmth and wealth of love and happiness. All joy and bounty seemed to be His. His presence brought a sunshine in which fears and sorrows melted and lost their power. He was always their Master, their Lord, their Leader. His heart, His mind, outreached their range on every side. His sweetness and charm and wisdom and knowledge seemed boundless. His goodness and holiness awed them. But though they felt themselves immeasurably beneath Him, and He in His greatness remote, afar, yet they knew He loved to be with them; He loved to praise them; they had never had so true, so dear a friend on earth as this Jesus; and however exalted in reality He might be, yet He drew them to Him more and more and in His companionship they expanded and matured.

With complete detachment they devoted themselves to His service. They left their homes. They abandoned their positions. They scattered north, south, east, west, spreading their message from God of love and joy and hope. He had promised: '*lo, I am with you alway.*' (Matt. xxviii 20.) Yes, He was in their hearts never to be parted from them, and now they need ask nothing of the world for He Himself was with them—and He, their own Beloved, was the Son of God.

They were as sheep in the midst of wolves, advocates of peace in a world that gloried in war, of justice and mercy in a civilisation founded on conquest and slavery, of unity when men and nations cherished their divisions, votaries of a universal God of love in an age of a thousand fratricidal hates. Gladly they welcomed toil and hardship, calumny, persecution, loneliness; through suffering they drew nearer to their Master's presence. No doubt dwelt in their minds. They were as men walking in the glory of the sunshine through a city of the blind.

When He had been taken from them and they had gained from the strong faith of Mary an acuter insight into heavenly things, and began to recognise the greatness of their Lord's exaltation, they reached new degrees of self-surrender untouched before. As days and months of faithful fearless witness to Him went by, their enthralment and their adoration deepened. With wondering, throbbing hearts they entered into the mystery of His pronouncement: '*Before Abraham was, I am.*' (John viii. 58.) They felt that in Him was being made manifest to them the image of a mystic Divine Spirit, the Truth of Truth, the Word that was in the beginning with God, that was God, the Word without Whom nothing was made that was made, the Word that now was continuing His creative work and bringing into being a new creature, a new degree of manhood, a new and more abundant life than men had before enjoyed.

A deep content, a deep happiness was theirs. In the morning they woke to it, and at night they carried it into their sleep. 'Lo, I am with you always,' said Christ; and He was faithful Who promised. The earth indeed was at the moment in the grasp of His enemies. Those who knew Him and loved Him were few, persecuted, powerless. But His ultimate and complete victory was assured, was near. Their special privilege and glory it was to prepare the world for the Great Day of His conquest and to make the people worthy to meet Him when He came.

All through the Old Testament had run a thread of eager expectancy looking far out towards a Golden Age to come. The modern mind might recognise it as a dim awareness of man's progress towards an inevitable evolutionary goal. The Gospel did not allay this expectancy. On the contrary it confirmed and heightened it. It declared that this joyous and triumphant message of Love and Life was itself but a prelude. A greater message was to follow. For the first time in the history of Revelation a messenger of God made the intensifying of this age-old Expectancy the central feature of His teaching. The objective of all prophecy was but a step away, the promised Kingdom was at hand. The bounties and salvation brought to men by Christ was not the fullness of the Promise but rather the channel and the power through which man would be made strong enough to receive the crowning blessedness of Unity.

The nature of that blessedness was for the present to remain insensible. Its mysteries could not, as the Sacred Record shows, be made known by Christ even in private to His own chosen disciples; they must be reserved for a future Revelation when the minds of men had been brought to maturity. Mankind must yet pass through direful afflictions and be brought near to destruction before, chastened by suffering, it emerged from the long cycle of Ignorance and Rebellion to the Haven of Perpetual Peace and Surrender to the Will of God. The careful study of Scripture with a spiritual mind will show every reader that the promised Kingdom would not appear on earth till after the Return of Christ and the coming of the Spirit of Truth. It was to be not spiritual only but material; not an individual achievement only but a collective; to rule over outward conditions of life as well as inward. In the complete loving obedience to the will of God which it would involve, prejudice between races, nations, and religions would be outgrown, justice and security would be established, war forgotten, mankind would become thoroughly unified, a system of universal responsiveness and co-operation would produce a new social order which would be maintained through new laws and new institutions.

That the Christ of the second coming, the Comforter, the Spirit of Truth, would bring a new, different, and more advanced Revelation, that He would have a new Mission, a distinct Function, is made by Christ and Holy Writ as clear as well can be. The whole narrative of the Scripture as illuminated by Bahá'u'lláh testifies to the error of the common Christian view that the Revelation given to the Jews in Palestine was terminal, that it imparted all the knowledge of God destined for mankind upon this planet, that the Second Coming of Christ would bring to the Christians nothing challenging nor new but would universally fix the Christian Faith as the one and only true Faith and would exalt those diverse and discordant dogmas, creeds, interpretations, rites, ceremonies, customs and observances which constitute what now is called Christianity to the throne of the world and abase all the other religions which have hitherto vied with it for the allegiance of mankind. How (it may well be asked) does this traditional expectation of the Churches differ in spirit from the calamitous superstition of Scribe and Pharisee about their Messiah? How does it differ in spirit from the orthodox view of the Muslim concerning Muḥammad as the 'Seal of the Prophets'?

Nowhere is it suggested that even the establishment of the Kingdom of God and the fulfilment of all the prophecies of the two Testaments will bring the close of the evolutionary unfolding of man's heart and soul and the end of Revelation. Who could doubt that when God's victory is complete, when harmony between His will and man's has been attained, when the meek have inherited the earth and the righteous are enthroned, man's intellectual and moral progress will go forward more rapidly than ever and will continue indefinitely? The Bahá'í Faith teaches expressly that this is the fact, and opens a prospect of man's individual evolution through many aeons ahead under the sacred guidance of a succession of High Prophets.

It was not however to the further unfolding of man's

powers but rather to the actual coming of the Kingdom, to the dangers of the Advent of the New Messenger from God that Christ drew the attention of the apostles and of posterity. This Advent would be wholly different from Christ's personal presence either in a believer's heart or in the midst of a gathering of two or three of the faithful. If He said on the one side 'I am with you always even to the end of the Age', he said on the other 'I will come again': two distinct promises. The Second Coming would be a dated historical event, the time and hour of which were already known to the Father. It would have a material as well as a spiritual side, and would follow the pattern of other manifestations. The Prophet, for all His glory and sovereignty would, when He appeared, be an ordinary man, like everyone else about Him—as Abraham had been, or Moses or Jesus Christ Himself. His appeal would be to the detached heart, to the spiritual mind. He would not coerce belief by any outward display of divine majesty, any more than Jesus had done. His coming would be (like that of Jesus) a test, to distinguish the worthy from the unworthy, the righteous from the unrighteous. It might happen that an unbelieving mankind might not recognise the Divine Judgment that was being passed upon them. It might even be that professing Christians might not know their Lord when He came back. He plainly indicated indeed that this would occur, when He pictured Himself at the Great Assize pronouncing to those who used His Name but did not do His works the dreadful sentence 'I never knew you'.

He foretold that affliction such as had never been known before nor ever would be known again would fall upon mankind before the final Redemption of the race. But on this Second Coming He would be invested with what no earlier Prophet had had—power to enforce the Rule of God on earth, to overwhelm the resistance of the forces of evil, to put down all rebellion and establish on an impregnable basis the dominion of God in the hearts of men and in the outward conditions of life upon the planet.

He promised His disciples—who can have little realised to what He referred—that the Gates of Hell would not prevail, that the meek should inherit the earth, assured them that it was their Father's good pleasure to give them the Kingdom and that in it the righteous should shine forth as the sun.

The long reign of Darkness was near an end. The Day was at hand: the Day of God on which should fall no night!

This Faith in the coming victory of God; the vision of their Risen Lord riding forth conquering and to conquer in the final battle for Righteousness and Truth endued the early Christians with a power which nothing could gainsay or resist. So long as that faith and vision remained, that power never wholly failed the Christian Church.

When those who would bring the canon of Christian Scripture to a close sought a befitting climax to that majestic story of the spiritual evolution of the race, they chose the Apocalypse of St. John the Divine in which is depicted with a glowing love and an ecstasy of faith that has charmed the heart and enthralled the imagination of the faithful down all the ages, the final triumph of the cause of Christ and God on earth. Here in prophetic symbol the Seer of old time portrays the spiritual history of the days in which we now are living, recounts the mission and the achievement of the Báb and of Bahá'u'lláh, and spreads in golden words before our eyes the glory of the Dawning Day of God which for a hundred years has shone on all mankind, though seen of none save those in whom had returned the spirit of the early founders of our faith.

'And the angel which I saw stand upon the sea and upon the earth lifted up his hand to heaven, and sware by him that liveth for ever and ever . . . (that) in the days of the voice of the seventh angel, when he shall begin to sound, the mystery of God should be finished, as he hath declared to his servants the prophets.' (Rev. x. 5–7.)

'And the same hour was there a great earthquake, and the tenth part of the city fell, and in the earthquake were slain of men seven thousand: and the remnant were affrighted, and gave glory to the God of heaven. The second woe is past; *and*, behold, the third woe cometh quickly. And the seventh angel sounded; and there were great voices in heaven, saying, the kingdoms of this world are become *the kingdoms* of our Lord, and of his Christ; and he shall reign for ever and ever.' (Rev. xi. 13–15.)

'And I saw a new heaven and a new earth: for the first heaven and the first earth were passed away; and there was no more sea.

'And I John saw the holy city, new Jerusalem, coming down from God out of heaven, prepared as a bride adorned for her husband.

'And I heard a great voice out of heaven saying, Behold, the tabernacle of God *is* with men, and he will dwell with them, and they shall be his people, and God himself shall be with them, *and be* their God.

'And God shall wipe away all tears from their eyes; and

there shall be no more death, neither sorrow, nor crying, neither shall there be any more pain: for the former things are passed away.' (Rev. xxi. 1–4.)

'And he carried me away in the spirit to a great and high mountain, and shewed me that great city, the holy Jerusalem, descending out of heaven from God,

'Having the glory of God: and her light *was* like unto a stone most precious, even like a jasper stone, clear as crystal . . .' (Rev. xxi. 10–11.)

'And he shewed me a pure river of water of life, clear as crystal, proceeding out of the throne of God and of the Lamb.

'In the midst of the street of it, and on either side of the river, *was there* the tree of life, which bare twelve *manner of* fruits, *and* yielded her fruit every month: and the leaves of the tree *were* for the healing of the nations.

'And there shall be no more curse: but the throne of God and of the Lamb shall be in it; and his servants shall serve him:

'And they shall see his face; and his name *shall be* in their foreheads.

'And there shall be no night there; and they need no candle, neither light of the sun; for the Lord God giveth them light: and they shall reign for ever and ever.' (Rev. xxii. 1–5.)

EPILOGUE

Out of that Gospel, and in the hope of the Coming of the Kingdom of God on earth there arose in Europe a mighty civilisation which called itself by the name of Christ and carried the Christian message around the globe. It reached an unparalleled degree of prestige, of power, and prosperity. Its industry, commerce and finance overshadowed the rest of the planet. It was the fountain-head of the science, the culture, the political ideas which exercised unchallenged supremacy over mankind.

In the eighteenth century the great historian Gibbon, in prophetic mood, sketched the prospect which he then saw before his country.

> ... in war, the European forces are exercised by temperate and undecisive contests ... The balance of power will continue to fluctuate, and the prosperity of our own or the neighbouring kingdoms may be alternately exalted or depressed; but these partial events cannot essentially injure our general state of happiness, the system of arts, and laws, and manners, which so advantageously distinguish, above the rest of mankind, the Europeans and their colonies.*

When, some hundred years later, a scholar-statesman reminded his fellow citizens that they were the most

* *The History of the Decline and Fall of the Roman Empire*, ch. XXXVIII *ad finem*.

enlightened generation of the most enlightened age in history, or an illustrious proconsul wrote that the political system to which he belonged 'is under Providence the most beneficent institution which the world has ever seen . . ., and its work in the Far East is not yet accomplished', they did but record the general impression of the time. At the opening of the twentieth century, the West believed that through the guidance of Reason and of Science its security and continued advance in wealth and power was assured. It regarded the Order it had established as the apex of the entire process of human history and as synonymous with civilisation itself. In its religious aspect, its many churches were thought to represent the Kingdom of God and the success of their foreign missions was expected in due time to inaugurate the reign of God on earth.

Then suddenly in an hour when they looked not, taking them unawares, catching them as it were in a snare from which there was no escape, the floods of human hate and jealousy and greed were let loose. The whole vast system began to disintegrate. Its strength, its glory, its dominion, its pride and affluence passed away—not through the impact of a foreign foe as in the case of ancient Rome or Jerusalem, nor through any external influence, but through some undiagnosed disease within its own system. Statesman, philosopher, scientist, scholar and divine, all were at a loss. None could tell whence the visitation came nor whither it would lead. None could shore up the tottering structure of the social order, nor check the ever-extending process of decay and dissolution.

The earnest and open-minded Christian saw that the

foundations of Church and State were gone. Religion had become a collection of forms, phrases and customs which men borrowed from their predecessors or from their environment. The disputations of rival sects proved that the teaching which in its purity had been the cause of concord, union and progress, had changed its character and become the cause of discord, of division and of immobility. Leaders of the Faith when asked for the light and guidance it was their business to give showed neither vision nor foresight nor initiative nor constructive power: they would give such an answer as would sustain their own prestige or protect some man-made tradition which they served. The Gospel, as divines interpreted it, had become irrelevant. Love had long since grown cold. Faith was but the shadow of a name. Men watched no longer for the coming of the Kingdom of God. Their eyes were fixed in helpless horror on the opening gates of hell. The Christian looks eastward at the other world-faiths, sisters of his own faith. He looks at the cults, worships, mysticisms, ideologies that beset his path. He sees that all is vanity. The shadow of spiritual death lies over the whole wide world. Search as he will, he finds nothing to win the allegiance of his heart and spirit, no hope, no vision that resembles Christ's glorious pattern of the future of redeemed mankind—till the day when there breaks upon his soul the dawning splendour of the Revelation of Bahá'u'lláh.

There within the Bahá'í Faith the spirit of the early Christian Church has risen again. There stand the great essentials—spirituality, love, reverence, obedience. There the Gospel standards of loyalty and faith are restored in their fullness. Christ is adored as the very Word of God, sharing God's glory from all eternity. Faith is not a profession, nor an imitation, but is as that of Peter described by Christ—'*flesh and blood hath not revealed* it *unto thee, but my Father which is in heaven.*' True membership is tested as Christ prescribed; '*By this shall all* men *know that ye are my disciples, if ye have love one to another*', and '*If ye love me, keep my commandments*'*—tested and proved that is by obedience to Christ and love to one another. Christ's message is renewed, elucidated, expanded, carried forward. The Gospel (along with the whole Bible) being explained in every point through a divine interpretation, it becomes once more a guide to truth and human life. Christ's crowning promise of the Kingdom, which the Churches have failed to realise and have for all practical purposes abandoned, stands in the Revelation of Bahá'u'lláh where in any Christian system it ought to stand, in the very centre, supplying the great objective of every Bahá'í endeavour as it once was the objective of the Apostles and their teaching.

Here he recognises the Return of Christ indeed, the Return of those qualities by which the Apostles identified Him on His first coming—His Return in spirit, in power, in His cause and purpose. The individual is different, the names and dates, ordinances and rites are changed. God now, as in the past, tests His creatures; He provides touchstones by which sincerity is tried. The external aspect of the teaching is changed that men's lack of insight may be exposed, and the continuity of bounties and blessings is hidden that only the true-hearted may discern it.

The Prophecies are fulfilled! The Promises one and all

* Matt. xvi. 17, John xiii. 35, and John xiv. 15.

in their fullness have been kept! The Ancient Faith of all the ages is vindicated! The Call of Christ is heard through all the earth summoning His faithful ones to join the Legions of Light and work in the Name of Bahá'u'lláh for the prosperity and salvation of mankind and the establishment of the Kingdom of God on earth.

And this volume on the Bible and the Bahá'í Faith is issued that Christians everywhere, following the Guidance of the Gospel, may pass into the Bahá'í community, may hear the promised words spoken to them '*Come, ye blessed of my Father, inherit the kingdom prepared for you from the foundation of the world*', and may at once arise for the regeneration of the human race.

THE AUTHOR

GEORGE TOWNSHEND was born in Dublin and educated at Uppingham and Hertford College, Oxford, taking a Classics degree in 1899. While reading at the King's Inns for the Irish Bar, he became a leader-writer on the Irish Times. After being called he travelled in the United States and in 1906 was ordained a priest of the Protestant Episcopal Church in St. Mark's Cathedral, Salt Lake City, Utah. Four years later he joined the staff of the University of the South, Sewanee, Tennessee, and before long was appointed Assistant Professor of English.

After the outbreak of war, in 1916 he returned home and entered the service of the Church of Ireland. At this time, through an American friend, he came into touch with 'Abdu'l-Bahá, with whom he had a correspondence and whose life and teaching made on him an immediate and lasting impression. In 1919 he took up residence as Rector of Ahascragh, a country parish in County Galway. He spent his leisure there in the study of comparative religion and in the writing of his books *The Altar on the Hearth, The Genius of Ireland, The Promise of All Ages* and *The Heart of the Gospel*. (Parts of the first two he later included in The Mission of Bahá'u'lláh.) In 1933 he was elected a Canon of St. Patrick's Cathedral, Dublin, and also in that year became Archdeacon of Clonfert.

Mr Townshend's earnest wish was to bring his church 'under the heavenly Jerusalem', a hope expressed to him by 'Abdu'l-Bahá. After three decades he resigned his Orders in 1947 and transferred his residence to Dublin, where he and his family became foundation members of the first Bahá'í Spiritual Assembly. 'I feel I must make any sacrifice,' he wrote to the Bishop of Utah, 'in order to be free to help in transmitting to my fellow-Christians a Message which presents the one and only hope of respiritualising mankind and rebuilding the social order'.

In 1951 Mr Townshend was one of the first to be appointed by the Guardian of the Bahá'í Faith a Hand of the Cause during his lifetime. Though his physical health gradually weakened, he greatly inspired the Bahá'ís of the British Isles and many others who met him. When seventy-eight years of age he began the project nearest to his heart – the writing of *Christ and Baha'u'llah* – bringing it, despite incredible handicaps, to completion and publication in the month of his death, March 1957. The Guardian, in a cable, extolled 'his sterling qualities, his scholarship, his challenging writings . . . his fearless championship Cause he loved so dearly. . .'

The core of Mr. Townshend's vision was that human history is 'an epic written by the finger of God. . . and there is no race nor nation nor tribe nor even individual who has not a designated place in the unfolding of the Grand Design of God'. He has left a body of writing which clearly delineates this vision and will continue to inform and challenge readers for generations to come.

A biography of George Townshend written by David Hofman is published by George Ronald.